AQUARIAN
BOOK CENTRE
26 VAN DER MERWE STREET
HILLBROW 2001   TEL: 642-5829

OMNI-COSMICS:
Miracle Power
Beyond the Subconscious

ANN FISHER

PARKER PUBLISHING COMPANY, INC. • WEST NYACK, N.Y.

© 1979 by

Parker Publishing Company, Inc.
West Nyack, New York

All rights reserved. No part of this book may be reproduced in any form or by any means, without permission in writing from the publisher.

This book is a reference work based on research by the author. The opinions expressed herein are not necessarily those of or endorsed by the publisher.

Library of Congress Cataloging in Publication Data

Fisher, Ann
   Omni-cosmics.

   1. Success. 2. Psychical research. I. Title.
BJ1611.2.F55   131'.32   78-25753
ISBN 0-13-634188-8

Printed in the United States of America

To

WALTER B. GIBSON —

A great writer and friend, who
inspired me to write this book

What This Book Can Do For You

What do you want in life?

You have unlimited psychic miracle power—power beyond the subconscious mind—within you, there for the tapping. This book will give you the techniques that will turn on this power force so you can use this energy to get all you want in life.

This miracle power is *Omni-Cosmics*—the source of universal power that lies beyond the subconscious.

Modern scientists have not recognized this universal power within man yet. But the leaders in the ancient world knew and used the secrets which will be revealed to you in this book. I know because I have researched this hidden knowledge for 15 years and traveled to the ends of the earth for them.

I will show you how to tap the unlimited powers of your own mind. This is what Omni-Cosmics really is. It will enable you to perform so-called impossible feats. You will be able to attain a paradise on earth for yourself and all those you love.

This universal mind power is ready to respond to your command. You cannot see it, but you can sense it and feel it when it starts to open up for you.

Suddenly your dreams come true. It is like a miracle.

You can grasp this hidden energy power and accomplish anything you set out to do.

You will find you have so much power within . . . . It just lies there available for the asking . .

Through the universal laws that I reveal in this book you will find you have an Aladdin's lamp, for you can ask your Magic Sage to do your bidding to bring to you all you desire.

You do not have to depend on luck anymore. The storehouse of mental energy is at your fingertips. It is within you. Your mental energy can give you all you want in this universe . . .

Are you disappointed in love? Do you need money to pay up your bills? Is your health poor? Do you feel your world is closing in on you? Do you feel you are not getting ahead in life? Do you feel everyone is against you? Would you like to know what the future has to offer for you? Would you like to change your destiny?

If so, this book will show you the methods that will change your life. Start today to look ahead and reach out to the Omni-Cosmic Universal Laws and bring all your desires and dreams within your reach.

By the time you finish the last chapter of this book you will know the way and you will bring these changes about suddenly.

You can reshape your future. I did.

For a number of years I saw people who were overwhelmingly successful. They obtained anything they wanted. I asked myself, "What is the secret of their success? If they could do it, why can't I?" I started to meditate and became engrossed in the occult. In this way I found there were definite ways to master and change my destiny. Then the secrets were unfolded to me. It was so simple I was amazed . . Why did I wait so long?

I know my methods work. Countless numbers of my students testify to this. The methods I have included in this book are easy to apply and simple to understand.

There are miracles ahead for you. Just start reading and following my directions and you will be happier and more successful than you would dream possible.

I DID IT—SO CAN YOU

A few years ago I was an unknown person, working eight hours a day in an office that I disliked and putting up with a boss who was a tyrant. I never had enough money after payday to buy the luxuries I desired. My health was poor. I did not own a car. I lived in a section of the city I disliked, but it was all I could afford.

In my spare time, I became interested in the occult and started to study its principles and search out its secrets. Gradually I

What This Book Can Do For You 7

found some ancient teaching that I could adapt to my life. I found the secrets that changed my life and those secrets are in this book in simple, easy-to-understand language.

In a matter of less than two years I went from being an unknown person to become a well-known personality, first in my local area and the following year to a national level. I went from poverty to a high income, literally from rags to riches. I never look back. I always look ahead to greater things in life, anticipating that the best is yet to come.

Now I drive a new golden Cadillac which to a Leo is an image of success and radiance. I have appeared on TV and radio countless times across the U.S. and Canada. I now have money in the bank and own blue chip stocks that will be going up in the coming years.

This year I bought a house on the most expensive street in my city. Also the same year I moved my office into the most impressive office building in my area.

I was ill with asthma. This was caused by not being able to get what I wanted—like being choked—but now my health is perfect. Everything in my life has changed for the best. I was unlucky in love,—but now I have a perfect mate.

You will call it a miracle. I say I learned these magic secrets *of Omni-Cosmic Power* and adapted them to my everyday life.

Remember you can do this also.

POWER BEYOND THE SUBCONSCIOUS

This is the power used by the ancients who had greater knowledge than modern man gives them credit for. It is the power to generate what you want by saying the right Omni-Cosmic rituals. It is the "power of the universe."

In ancient teachings from Egypt, India and Tibet, I found these secrets and this book will show you how simple they are to use to get what you want in life.

In ancient times only the high priests or a limited few knew this knowledge.

All of us possess Omni-Cosmic Psychic Power, another name for power beyond the subconscious. Look around you, for it is always available. The power is not new, but it is there. Press that power button and see what begins to happen. You will be amazed. You will not have to take second place to anyone in life.

You will turn on your Omni-Cosmic Psychic Power Channel using your psychic abilities such as clairvoyance, automatic writing, astral projection, seeing auras, psychometry, telepathy or perhaps psychokinesis (the ability to control matter with your mind). You will learn the secrets of the soul. You will learn more about reincarnation by knowing what your soul has been through in past lives.

You will look into your magic mirror and find what you are seeking; lost articles and lost people, wealth and power, love and companionship, and you will find the key to perfect living. As you gaze into your magic mirror your past lives may unfold before your eyes.

You will be able to contact people and see beyond walls for great distances.

I promise you that this book will help you realize your limitless powers. You will be able to use your Omni-Cosmic Power Channel to its fullest range throughout the universe.

Cease looking outside yourself, for you possess this power within. You just have to press the right button.

Tap the Omni-Cosmic Power instantly for it responds at once. This power was sought by occultists, warlocks, witches and alchemists during ancient as well as modern times. The right ritual starts the action and away you go on to success and fulfillment.

You can do this regardless of your education, race, religion or position in life.

It is my purpose to enlighten you on these rituals of how to tap the Omni-Cosmic Psychic Energy so you will find all you seek in life.

I feel I have lived in ancient times and had this knowledge for when I began my research it seemed that many things were familiar. Your past lives are stored in the superconscious mind and this is what I tapped. I feel I was supposed to give this to the world now. The times are right for people to use and accept this occult knowledge.

SOME THINGS THIS BOOK WILL HELP YOU TO DO

Attain your ideal weight like magic.

Bring in endless streams of wealth so you can live like a king.

Build a wall of protection around your mind and body that will shield you from harm.

Find the perfect mate and achieve marital happiness.

Learn to control the thoughts of others.

Locate lost articles and people.

Get that promotion you want at work.

Repeal a black magic or voodoo attack.

Open locked doors.

Travel astrally and break the wall of time.

Read other persons' minds and know their hidden ideas and secrets.

Turn your thoughts and wishes into solid material things by using Omni-Cosmic Photography.

Look years younger through Omni-Cosmic Psychics.

Break bad habits such as drinking and smoking.

Win money in a lottery or horse race.

Call on your spirit loved ones on the other side to show you the future.

Use your Omni-Cosmic Healing Buttons for instant healing.

THEY DID IT—SO CAN YOU

Jerry gets $10,000 from worthless land

Jerry needed $10,000 badly for his business. It was sink or swim if he did not come up with the money. By using my Money Magnetism Ritual he received some money for land he had owned for a long time, but considered worthless.

What he did was to tap his inner mind to stir up his Omni-Cosmic energy forces so that a company came to him to buy the land and thus saved him from financial ruin.

You will be able to produce money from "out of thin air" as Jerry did.

Remember nothing is impossible with Omni-Cosmic power.

Money appears out of nowhere

Mary A. needed money for taxes. She was quite upset and feared she would lose her home if she could not come up with the money.

I told her to use the Money Visualize Ritual for help. She did and found a winning lottery ticket on the street just weeks later. It was exactly the amount she needed to pay the taxes and save her home.

Mary sent her Omni-Cosmic Psychic Electrons into action for help and she got a response within a short time.

John bought a lottery ticket for $1,000 a week for life and won

John R., a factory worker was desperately in need of money for his rent, car payments and a pile of bills that were stacked up on his desk at home. He used the Omni-Cosmic Magic Sage Ritual and two months later bought the winning lottery ticket that paid $1,00 a week for life.

His Magic Sage told him what day to buy the ticket and the store to purchase it in.

It was a happy ending to a sad story.

Grace finds a husband through Omni-Cosmic Psychic Photography

Grace D. was 35, unmarried and quite unhappy for she felt no man would ever want her. She started to project the type of man she would like to marry on her mental screen.

Within a month she met a man in a restaurant who fit the one she had projected in her mind. They married within seven months and they have been happy ever since.

Samantha lost 95 pounds and found a husband

Samantha J. was 235 pounds, 29 years old and had never had a date in her life. She was frustrated and resigned to her dull life.

She used her OCP ritual for miraculous weight control and lost 95 pounds in the next six months. Shortly thereafter she met a young man whom she married within ten months. Samantha is a new person, full of life and love and has created a new image of herself.

Carol repels a Black Magic attack

Carol J, a professor at one of the local colleges where I live, was sent a negative charge from a student she had failed in one of her classes.

Carol's health, career, and family ties were threatened by his black magic attack. She used her Omni-Cosmic Protecto-Ray three times a day for a week. She sent the evil back to the student who had sent it out to her in the first place.

Carol did this for one week and a dramatic change occurred in her personal life which was all positive. She was able to clear up all the negative vibrations sent to her.

Michael, the student who had sent out the Black Magic Attack had a car accident within 10 days. It sent him to the hospital for three weeks. While he was in the hospital his apartment had a fire and he lost all of his possessions.

He learned the price he paid was too dear to play around with negative forces again.

The blind made to see

Alice T, had been blind since the age of 12. I felt she became blind immediately after her father's death due to a guilt feeling. I told her to use her Omni-Cosmic Psychic Buttons to open up her sight again and it did so within three months.

The powerful words in her OCP ritual released her from the bondage of being sightless that had been caused by her negative thinking. She was healed by her positive attunement through Omni-Cosmic Healing Power.

She thanks her lucky stars she found how to tap in on OCP.

These are just a few of the many cases of people who were helped through OCP.

WHY DOESN'T EVERYONE USE THIS INCREDIBLE POWER SOURCE

You may ask, "Why doesn't everyone use this OCP source if it is so easy to use?" This is because so many people fear the unknown or occult forces.

We are a product of our environment and past conditioning. This country was settled by Puritans who felt the psychic was witchcraft or of the devil. We are slowly moving into the new psychic age.

There is nothing to fear about Omni-Cosmic Power for it is within and around us. Once you discover it you will find there is nothing spooky about it. You are just using the laws of the universe.

This book gives the secrets to this new personal power. You will not sneer at the occult once you find out its secrets.

THIS IS THE TIME TO WAKE UP YOUR OMNI-COSMIC PSYCHIC POWER

This book has been written with every word carefully chosen to sink into your subconscious mind. Remember you are what your mind thinks you are. Thoughts produce the action. You have to say the right words to get the right reaction from the universe.

This book can do all this for you if you follow and use the Omni-Cosmic Psychic Rituals. Your life pattern will take a new turn on the road to success and accomplishment. You will be victorious by finding a life that is more rewarding.

If you have the desire, the results will be so great and far reaching that you will wonder why you did not discover the secrets before.

Your mind is your most powerful instrument. Just send out the right mental command which will be projected on your mind screen and magnified many times, producing all you send it.

I promise you that you can have anything in life. So start today and you will be happy you did.

Read a few minutes each day and the mighty Omni-Cosmic Power Machine within you will answer your commands.

Use this occult knowledge wisely for both yourself and your fellowman and you will be rewarded many times over.

Life will be exciting and be worth living to its fullest.

I so declare it.

Ann Fisher

Contents

What This Book Can Do For You 5

1. **Commanding Miracles by Tuning in to Your Power Beyond the Subconscious** 19

   You Have This Invisible Power Within You . Tuning in on Your Omni-Cosmic Power Channel . Protection Ritual for Traveling . I Did It—So Can You . Money Ritual for Finding a Job . Love Ritual to Contact Your Loved One . Love Attraction Ritual

2. **Tapping Your Omni-Cosmic Psychic Wealth Miracle Generator for Money Magnetism** 35

   How to Activate It . Anyone Can Start the Money Flow . Money Magnetism Ritual . Money Visualization Ritual . Give Some of the Money to Help Humanity . Job-Finding Ritual . Thoughts Mean Action—Action Means Results

3. **How to Use Omni-Cosmic Psychic Power for Instant Healing** 48

   Steps in Healing Your Body . Push Your Omni-Cosmic Healing Buttons . Start the Day with the Perfect Health Ritual . Command Yourself to Be Healed . Block out Negative Words

4. **Tuning in to Omni-Cosmic Psychic Airwaves to Control the Thoughts of Others and Find the Ideal Mate** 62

   You Have Hidden Powers Within . Using Your Omni-Cosmic Eye Command . Using Omni-Cosmic

Contents

Gestures . You Can Contact the Subconscious Mind When the Other Person Sleeps . Your Mind Will Find Your Perfect Mate

5. Using Your Omni-Cosmic Psychometrics for Finding Lost People and Treasure 74

Developing Omni-Cosmic Psychometrics . You Can Pick up Vibrations from Your City or Town . How to Find Lost People . Tune in to Find Lost Treasure, Water or Precious Stones

6. Enveloping Yourself in an Omni-Cosmic Protecto-Ray to Ward off Anybody or Anything Standing in the Way of Miracles You Deserve 82

The Truth About Psychic Assault . How to Build a Thought Wave Alarm . How to Turn on Your Omni-Cosmic Protecto-Ray

7. How to Call Your Omni-Cosmic Magic Sage to Be Your Willing Invisible Slave 92

Power Words to Summon Your Magic Sage . How to Talk to Your Magic Sage

8. Using Omni-Cosmic Psychometrics to Revitalize the New You for Better Health and Happiness 102

The Secret of Psychometrics for Health . Use Your Wake-up Psychometrics . Psychometrics Chants for Health . How to Break down Negative Programming Through Omni-Cosmic Psychometrics

9. Obtaining Miracles of Wealth, Personal Command, and Joy Through Omni-Cosmic Psychic Photography ..111

How Soon Can You Expect Results? . You Can Achieve Happiness . Success with Omni-Cosmic Photography . Psychic Photography Can Break Old Habits . Start the Day with a Happy and Peaceful Mental Picture

10. Using Your Omni-Cosmic Psychic Rays to Achieve
Endless Streams of Wealth 120

You Can Become as Wealthy as You Wish . How to Turn
on Your Omni-Cosmic Psychic Rays for Wealth . Use
Omni-Cosmic Cablegrams for Luck and Success

11. How Omni-Cosmic Psychometrics Can Reveal
Miraculous Instant Answers in Dreams
and Visions 130

Omni-Cosmic Psychometrics Will Make Your Dreams
Come True . Great Men of History Used Omni-Cosmic
Psychometrics to Obtain Their Dreams . Omni-Cosmic
Psychometrics Can Give You an Answer Quickly .
Program Your Mind for Psychic Answers . Dreams Can
Reshape Your Future

12. Omni-Cosmic Psychometrics Can Materialize
Miraculous Riches You Desire Through
Using Omni-Cosmic Telegrams 142

Seven Omni-Cosmic Telegrams That Will Start Your OCP
Power Functioning . Create Your Future . Challenge
Yourself . Project Your Will . Decree Positive
Commands That Will Come to Pass . Use Your Omni-
Cosmic Telegram to Find Your Greatest
Accomplishments . Become a Winner in Life

13. Looking into the Future with Omni-Cosmic Psychic
Power for Rewards Now! 153

Is It Possible to See into the Future? . Your Magic Sage
Will Show You the Future . How to Determine Time in a
Future Situation . In Time You Will Not Need Your
Magic Sage to See the Future

14. Using Omni-Cosmics to Travel Astrally to Discover
Miraculous Secret Knowledge and
Break the Time Barrier 164

What Happens When You Travel Astrally . How to
Travel Astrally Using Omni-Cosmics . It Is Easy to See
Places You Have Never Been to

Contents 17

15. Using Omni-Cosmic Physchic Imagonics to See Through the Magic Mirror for Love, Power, Money, Health and Happiness 174

    How to Use Psycho-Imagonics with Your Magic Mirror . Your Magic Mirror Opens up New Pathways

16. Tapping the Omni-Cosmic Power Channel to Release Miraculous Protective Psychic Powers 184

    How to Release Your Protective Psychic Powers . Help Comes from the Fourth Dimension . Turn on Your Omni-Cosmic White Pillar of Light . Ritual for White Pillar of Light

17. Using Omni-Cosmic Power for Miraculous Weight Control and for More Youthful Energy 194

    Forget Your Early Programming . Learn to Work with Yourself . You Will Overcome the Habit of Overeating . "Yes" Foods versus "No" Foods . How to Turn on Your Omni-Cosmic Power for Weight Loss . Change Your Sandwich Habit

18. Omni-Cosmic Psychics Can Release Your Full Mental Powers for Greater Health and Success 208

    Meditation Is Very Important . Show the Right Reaction . Ritual for Ridding Yourself of Negative Thoughts . The Power of Suggestion Is Long-Lasting . Look at Yourself in a New Way . Meditation Is the Key to What you Seek in Life . Rejuvenate Your Body and Mind Through Omni-Cosmic Psychics . Live Your Life to the Fullest

19. Using Omni-Cosmic Telepathic Power to Reveal Hidden and Secret Things to You Automatically! 223

    Tap into Your Power Source to Know the Secret, Hidden Things in a Person's Mind . Learn to Read the Thoughts of a Person Near You—or at a Distance . Build a Mental Wall Around Your Mind So No One Can Penetrate It . You Can Break Through Time and Space with OCT

Power . How to Contact Departed Loved Ones or Great Men of the Past

20. Let Omni-Cosmic Psychic Power Reveal the Never-Before-Unlocked Secrets of the Ages 234

What Is Omni-Cosmic Soul Attainment? . Money Is Not the Only Answer for Happiness . You Will Benefit from Knowledge of Past Lives . How to Find Total Contentment and Happiness in Your Life

Chapter 1

Commanding Miracles by Tuning in to Your Power Beyond the Subconscious

You have taken an important step in your life now. Wondrous things will begin to happen to you as you read this book.

A NEW FUTURE AWAITS YOU.

You are the MASTER OF YOUR OWN FUTURE and will soon DISCOVER THE NEW YOU.

To most people occult forces are mysterious and often feared, but when you discover that you have so much psychic power within, you will be amazed at the happiness that lies just ahead.

You live in a "Universe of Mystery" surrounded by invisible occult forces that mold and form our world.

In this modern psychic age man has attained things that seemed impossible in the last century. Scientists split the atom. Later we sent nine men to outer space and finally reached the moon. We proved man could overcome gravity by flying. We have radio and TV in almost every home in this country. There is so much more coming in this new and wondrous age. It is moving so fast that it is a thrilling experience to be a part of it.

As we see "Magic" is defined as, "A seeing control over natural forces through supernatural agencies."

YOU HAVE THIS INVISIBLE POWER WITHIN YOU

There is this power within all of us that can be stirred up and released; a power greater than you could ever fully realize.

William James, Father of Modern Psychology in America, stated that man uses only one-tenth of his mind power. Have you thought of all the power lying dormant within all of us? When you know how to tap this powerful force, miracles will occur in your life.

As you read from chapter to chapter new ideas and new energy will come. You will be a different person than you were when you first opened this book—a new you, a happier you, a more successful you.

In the ancient days of Atlantis, Egypt and Tibet, the privileged high priests and rulers knew how to tap this Omni-Cosmic Power Channel. Two years ago I was researching ancient material that had been willed to me by a friend who had done extensive research in ancient religions and magic.

Suddenly it became very clear to me that this power is so simple; yet the average man does not know how to tap its energy. The ancient priests knew how to get what they wanted from the Universal Mind. They carefully guarded this Omni-Cosmic Psychic Power for only a chosen few.

You can benefit from this mighty power force right now.

This power force is *within all of us.*

You will push the Omni-Cosmic Power Channel (OCPC) and a new life will unfold for you.

This OCPC is invisible, but there is no reason to doubt it. Love and joy cannot be seen, but you can feel them strongly when they are expressed. Radio and TV waves cannot be seen, but they do produce pictures and voices. All of these are produced by natural laws of the Infinite Mind.

Your future is *within you.*

TUNING IN ON YOUR OMNI-COSMIC MIRACLE POWER CHANNEL

Omni-Cosmic Miracle Power originates in your mind. Your brain is made of electrical and magnetic units that I call Omni-Cosmic Psychic Electrons. When your mind sends a command to the brain it stirs up these energy units and thus produces the results.

The Omni-Cosmic Psychic Energy can be tuned in with negative and positive charges that link with the Universal Mind. Your mind is like a tiny computer. You feed it information. Then an answer comes through. Every action that is sent it produces an opposite and equal reaction.

The process is simple. You learn to control the commands you send to your mind to get the Omni-Cosmic Psychic Electrons that give you positive results.

Remember you must send only positive charges and block out the negative ideas forever to get the proper tuning on your Omni-Cosmic Miracle Power Channel.

To activate your Omni-Cosmic Psychic Electrons you should learn how to meditate. Use the following program each day for 15 minutes, at the same time of day and in the same place in your home to get the best results. It is necessary to remove all tension so your Omni-Cosmic Psychic Energy will flow more freely. The more relaxed you become the more Omni-Cosmic Power is available for you.

USE THIS ACTION FORMULA FOR TUNING IN YOUR OMNI-COSMIC POWER CHANNEL

1. Relax your body in a comfortable chair sitting upright with your back supported.
2. Close your eyes and take your phone off the hook.
3. Dim the room, but have some light coming in.
4. Make your mind passive and direct your consciousness within.

Now that you have achieved the relaxed state say the following words to yourself slowly and let your subconscious mind direct what you are saying.

The power words to activate your Omni-Cosmic Power Channel are as follows:

Nam Yo Fara On **(pronounced exactly as written)—I direct my mind to relax my physical body. I feel a stillness within my whole body and mind. I am stilling my eyes and throat and nasal passages.**

I am stilling my lungs and chest. I am stilling my stomach and solar plexus.

I am stilling my hips and thighs. I am stilling my legs and feet.

I feel the stillness throughout my whole body. All tensions have gone and I am breathing easily and deeply. I seem to go deeper and deeper within myself.

My health and affairs are in perfect order and I love all those around me and wish them well.

I ask my deeper mind to assist me in all my undertakings today. I know, I believe and I will be more successful in all I do today and in the future.

Sit in this relaxed state for fifteen minutes. Draw a mental picture of what you want to achieve in your mind. See it as if it has already happened.

What you visualize in your mind will come to pass.

Through the proper tuning in on your Omni-Cosmic Psychic Wave Channel, mental energy, success, health and happiness will come to you. It is so simple and there within your reach.

A dream reveals the answer to Carolyn

Carolyn, a young secretary I know, had planned a trip to Europe in August, 1969. A week before she dreamed that she should cancel her trip and go the

Tuning in to Your Power Beyond the Subconscious 23

following month. When she awoke, she found herself upset and disturbed to such a degree that she canceled her trip the next day.

She told me later that before retiring on that particular day she had the dream, she asked herself, "Should I go at this time?" Her subconscious mind responded and sent her the answer.

Carolyn had used the Omni-Cosmic Power Channel ritual whenever she felt a need for an answer. This is the way the answer came to her in a dream state.

Carolyn rescheduled the trip the following month as she had been advised in the dream. Later on she found that the flight she was suppose to be on was hijacked. She would not have enjoyed the trip because the passengers were detained for a while and there was some unpleasantness in this delay.

Whenever you have a question you need an answer to, relax yourself, and mentally send yourself the question. You will receive a response within a short time. Your Omni-Cosmic Power Channel will go to work immediately to find the answer from the Universal Mind which knows all and sees all. It then transmits the message to you in the most effective psychic way it can.

When you are confused or pushing your mind too much you cannot get the response. You need to relax and wait for your Omni-Cosmic Power Button to flash in the answer.

"Omni" means "all or totally." "Cosmic" means "universal." When you meditate or pray or use my rituals you contact the Universal forces which are always present. They respond to you according to your belief in them.

Saved from a disturbing plane trip

Many people come to see me for a psychic consultation before going on a trip by air. I am able to tune in and feel if they should go on that particular day with the date and the flight number.

One day last fall, a client, Barbara R., came to see me and said, "I am going to Buffalo. Should I take the 6:00 P.M. or 7:07 P.M. flight?" My reply was, "I do not feel secure about the 7:07 P.M. flight. Do not take it, but go on the earlier flight."

Later I learned that the 7:07 P.M. flight had been hit by lightning and Barbara said, "Ann, if I had been on that plane, it would have been my last flight due to my fear of flying." The plane did not crash but the passengers were badly frightened.

Unlike Barbara, you cannot always find a psychic available to ask. You can ask your Omni-Cosmic Power Channel to tune in for you.

Whether you travel by plane, train or car or any other mode of transportation, you should always surround yourself with the Omni-Cosmic Protecto-Ray which I will describe in Chapter 6 of this book.

This is accomplished by visualization and the right words in the ritual. I always use it when I get into my car or any other vehicle I travel in. Then I can relax knowing that I have asked for safety and that I will get it. You can do this too.

OMNI-COSMIC PROTECTION RITUAL FOR TRAVELING

Nam Yo Fara On — Coe-Nah-Me-I-Mah, **Master Guide of the White Planes of the Spirit Realm protect this vehicle. I know that you are in contact with the Universal Mind that will protect me and everyone in this vehicle. I tune in my Omni-Cosmic Power Channel to the Universal Mind who is a living and powerful force. I will receive protection at all times when I ask for it.**

Tuning in to Your Power Beyond the Subconscious 25

I can feel and sense a shield of protection for I am surrounded by the Infinite Power of the Universe. All is well and I am safe.

After that you can sit back and enjoy the rest of your trip without fear. It really works for I can feel the shield around the vehicle when I have done this ritual.

I broke my accident record

Three times in three years, from 1965-1967, in the Sign of Aries The Ram (March 21 - April 20), I was parked for a red light and hit from behind by another car. My neck and back suffered a series of whiplashes which took their toll on my physical body.

When January of 1968 came around I was fearful that this accident pattern would happen again. I started to search for some guidance to save myself from another accident.

I sat and meditated using my Omni-Cosmic Power Channel to find some kind of an answer to my fears. The following Sunday in our local Spiritualist Church I received the following answer in a message from my dear departed grandfather who had passed on to the higher life ten years before. He said, "Ann, I know you need protection. Say the 91st Psalm everyday and you will get all the protection you need, my dear. You will be able to break the accident pattern you have experienced for the last three years." He also sent his love through the medium to me, my immediate family, and quickly departed.

When I returned home that Sunday I immediately went to my Bible, found the 91st Psalm and read it. I followed my grandfather's advice and read it everyday. When I did so I also visualized protection and I would feel an overshadowing protector around me.

I went through March and April of 1968 without an accident. I still carry a copy of the 91st Psalm at all times and I say it when I feel the need for protection. My prayers were answered. I have not had an accident since. Every time I get into my car I put the Omni-Cosmic Protecto-Ray around it to insure safety on the road. It has never failed me because when I use it I am sending positive energy out and using the right spirit force that is available to all.

Later in the year of 1968 I found a book, "Life Unlimited." *by F.L. Rawson who tells of a British Colonel Whittlesey who never lost a man in his regiment during World War II because he believed in the power of prayer. This was because all of his men cooperated and believed that they would be protected and they were.

Each day before breakfast each man recited the 91st Psalm. This programmed protection into their deeper minds and a response of protection was given.

Your Infinite Mind will answer you. All you have to do is ask and a response will be given.

THE 91ST PSALM

He who dwells in the shelter of the Most High, who abides in the Shadow of the Almighty.

I will say unto the Lord, "My refuge and my fortress: my God, in whom I trust."

For he will deliver you from the snare of the fowler and from the deadly pestilence;

He will cover you with his feathers, and under his wings you will find refuge:

His faithfulness is a shield and buckler.

---

*William Clowes and Son London, England

You will not fear the terror of the night, nor the arrow that flies by day, nor the pestilence that stalks in the darkness, nor the destruction that wastes at noonday.

A thousand may fall at your side, ten thousand at your right hand; but it shall not come nigh you.

You will only look with your eyes and see the recompense of the wicked.

Because you have made the Lord your refuge, the Most High your habitation, no evil shall befall you, no scourge come near your tent.

For he will give his angels charge over you to guard you in all your ways.

On their hands they will bear you up, lest you dash your foot against a stone.

You will tread on the lion and adder, the young lion and the serpent you will trample under foot.

Because he cleaves to me in love, I will deliver him:

I will protect him because he knows my name.

When he calls to me, I will answer him:

I will be with him in trouble.

I will rescue him and honor him.

With long life I will satisfy him, and show him my salvation.

I DID IT—SO CAN YOU

The universal power within us can direct the mind to action to perform everything you want in life. It is that mysterious force center in us that can be motivated by our minds that stirs up the energy forces to produce results.

You have this power source, so have I. You tap it by your thinking and using the Omni-Cosmic Rituals that I have included in this book.

Every day you should make it a practice to program yourself for positive benefits.

Since I have learned these secrets, I have been lucky, happy and very successful.

Roger found a job out of nowhere

Roger F, had been out of work for over ten months. He was very discouraged when he came to see me for a private consultation. I felt Roger would be able to get a job within a month if he would use my money ritual for finding a job.

Roger looked at me in amazement when I said this to him. He said he would do anything to get back to work. Bills had been piling up and he felt like a lost sheep.

I told him to turn on his Omni-Cosmic Power Channel first. Then he was to say the Omni-Cosmic Money Ritual three times a day, morning, noon and before going to sleep at night. He followed my instructions to the letter each day.

OMNI-COSMIC MONEY RITUAL FOR FINDING A JOB

Nam Yo Fara On, I ask my spirit forces within to find and direct my mind on a job that is right for me. I ask Ree-Ten-Oo-Toe, spirit of money to help me in this search. I will make myself available and direct all my energy to do my best to accomplish this. My Infinite Mind will help me in my search.

I believe it will come to me and I am ready to accept this new position. I believe, I believe, I believe.

Within a month, to be exact 28 days later, Roger received a call from a friend he had not heard from in two years who asked him if he wanted a job with his construction company. Roger knew his prayers were answered. He was filled with happiness and of course accepted the job offer. He is now a supervisor in this company.

Reunited with his financee

David S. was very unhappy because his fiancee had broken their engagement. David was in the Army, stationed in Germany, and was not able to get back to the States for another six months. He felt if he was closer to his girlfriend, Nancy, he could patch up their differences.

David wrote to me for help. I told him I felt there was hope for getting his fiancee back. I felt Nancy still loved him, but was confused at the present time. I gave him instructions on tuning his Omni-Cosmic Power Channel. Then I told him to say the Omni-Cosmic Lovers Ritual each day, morning and evening. It was best to do it upon arising and before he went to sleep at night. David did this faithfully for the next few weeks.

OMNI-COSMIC LOVE RITUAL TO CONTACT YOUR LOVED ONE

Nam Yo Fara On — I now tune my mind to Nancy whom I love and I know loves me also. I know our differences will be solved and our relationship will be the same as it was before — in love and happy with each other again.

Nancy loves me and I love her. I am sending her all my love today.

God's loving presence will guide me, uplift me and help me in my search for love and happiness. I know all is well and my heart is healed of all heartache and problems.

Within three weeks Nancy wrote to David and forgave him and they became engaged again. David was happy and in love. He realized that he had tuned into his Omni-Cosmic Power Channel which worked through to Nancy's mind and a response was given.

Bill finds the girl of his dreams

Bill M. had never had any love experiences with women because of his extreme shyness. He had supported his elderly parents until they died. All of his friends had married. He was a lonely bachelor of 38.

He came to see me about his future. I felt he would meet a woman and marry within the year. He said to me that he wished he could believe it, but it seemed impossible.

I told him to tune into the Omni-Cosmic Psychic forces and they would help him. He was to use the Omni-Cosmic Power Channel and the following Love attraction ritual. He was to say it three times a day to help him attract the right woman to him as soon as possible.

OMNI-COSMIC LOVE ATTRACTION RITUAL

"Nam Yo Fara On — I ask Ven-Or-Tur, spirit of love and happiness, to find the right woman for me to make my life happy. It will be a spiritual union with the Omni-Cosmic forces of the Universe. I know this woman exists and I will be directed to her. I believe, I believe, I believe. I leave it in your hands Ven-or-tur. So mote it be."

Within three months he met a woman who was 35 and also single. It was love from the start. Bill is no longer afraid of the future for he has found the woman of his dreams. They were married within the year and now have a fine marriage and two children.

His life worked out perfectly. He is so happy he found he could tap into the Omni-Cosmic forces for help.

June regained her youthful appearance through Omni-Cosmic Power

June E, a housewife and mother of three, was married to a well-to-do executive. Her husband traveled a great deal of the time on business and her children were now grown up and on their own. June needed something to help lift her spirits and brighten her outlook on life.

At 55, her age was showing. She knew she needed something to perk up her looks, to feel and look younger. She came to my office for direction.

I told her that by tuning into her Omni-Cosmic Miracle Power Channel she could, and would, find direction for her life ahead. I also felt she could reverse the aging process and bring back a more youthful appearance if she was happier and finding a place in life for herself.

June believed she could do this with some help. She was a very tense and nervous person. I felt that by relaxing and finding some new goals in life she would lose the wrinkles that were now there and thus look more youthful. Her aged look would disappear.

June tried tuning into her Omni-Cosmic Power Channel and within two months she looked and acted like a different person. June was younger looking, peppier and full of new ideas. She joined some new groups in her city and became more social. She was more reassured about herself by her new and younger appearance.

June was elected president of the woman's club in her city. She has been mentioned many times in the newspaper because of her work as president in the woman's club. She found a new life, happiness and a sense of being needed. This has changed her life for the best.

Remember, you are what your mind thinks you are.

PRACTICE OMNI-COSMICS MIRACLE POWER EVERY DAY

Stir up your Omni-Cosmic Psychic Electrons in your higher mind and get any answer you need by relaxing and knowing you will tap this mighty power force. An answer will come to you in accordance with your acceptancy of it.

You have a powerhouse of energy and force in your mind. Your subconscious mind can instantaneously contact that power source and give you all the help you want.

Your subconscious mind does have the ability to see all and know all, and you will receive a response.

Your mind must be quiet to receive all the answers. Every word or picture you send to your mind is recorded and will come to pass. It is necessary to send your mind only positive commands in order to get the best and avoid negative results.

Drop these words from your vocabulary—

NEVER, CANNOT, HATE, IMPOSSIBLE, MALICE

Replace with words like—

ALWAYS, POSSIBLE, GOOD, LOVE, ABUNDANCE, SUCCESS, PEACE

Remember "*Like attracts like*" and "*Birds of a feather flock together.*" Whatever you send out you get back. Send yourself the best, the positive and it will make your life successful.

As Shakespeare wrote so many years ago,

"*The fault, dear Brutus, is not in our stars,
But in ourselves, that we are underlings.*"

POINTS TO REMEMBER

1. Omni-Cosmic Psychic Power means communication with your Universal Mind or Spirit. Your subconscous mind directs the energy to release this power force within you.
2. "Magic" is being able to "control natural forces through supernatural agencies." Scientists do not know just what this force really is. We have an invisible power within us that knows all and sees all. You contact it with your conscious mind.
3. You can use this inner power to help find things that are lost, get answers to problems, find the right mate in life, obtain perfect health, buy the new home or car you always wanted through the proper conditioning you send it.
4. Omni-Cosmic Miracle Power originates in your mind. Your brain is made of electrical and magnetic units that I call Omni-Cosmic Psychic Electrons. To activate them you need to learn how to meditate, and should do this daily.
5. OCPC is invisible, but there is no reason to doubt it.
6. The power words to activate your Omni-Cosmic Power Channel are, "Nam Yo Fara On." When you say these words you tap the power source and energy starts to flow.
7. Think only positive thoughts. "You are what your mind thinks you are." Send the right commands for the best results.
8. You can be safe when traveling by sending out the right words and visual pictures. The Omni-Cosmic Protecto-Ray is always available. All you have to do is visualize it.
9. The 91st Psalm gives the necessary protection you need to avoid future accidents. Say it daily. Believe you are protected and you will be.
10. Whatever you imagine and feel to be true will come to pass with the proper tuning of your Omni-Cosmic Power Channel.
11. Reject negative words from your vocabulary. Replace them with positive words and your life will find a new direction full of happiness.

12. Remember, "Like attracts like" and "Birds of a feather flock together." Whatever you send out you get back.
13. As Shakespeare said so many years ago: *"The fault, dear Brutus, is not in our stars, But in ourselves, that we are underlings."*

Chapter 2

Tapping Your Omni-Cosmic Psychic Wealth Miracle Generator for Money Magnetism

You can have all the money you want.
Does this seem impossible? It is not.
This Omni-Cosmic power lies within you. There is a giant within you that will beckon to your call.
It is the subconscious mind which starts the Omni-Cosmic psychic power to generate the money flow to you when you need and desire it.
Nothing is too difficult.
You only have to ask and it will come.
Your dreams for a new car, a new home, a trip, new clothes will be fulfilled. You just have to send the right message to your subconscious mind for the results.

WEALTHY PEOPLE ARE NO DIFFERENT FROM YOU

First of all look around in your city or town for the person with the most money. Take a good look at this individual. Observe closely to see what he or she really looks like. See what color the hair and eyes are. Listen to the voice and analyze just what this person has that you do not have. It could be only money.

You will be surprised. There may be some qualities superior to yours, but in turn you may have other, far superior ones.

You must realize that the person is not that much different from you. If he has wealth, you can have it also. You can do just as he has done. The person is not that far superior, but for some reason has magnetized money while you have not.

First you must realize how much money you want. Then you must believe that you can magnetize it. All doubt must be removed. Faith is very important. Get yourself into the right frame of mind. Believe in your own capabilities. Remember, anything one person can do, you can do also.

HOW TO ACTIVATE YOUR PSYCHIC WEALTH MIRACLE GENERATOR

We all have our own Psychic Wealth Miracle Generator (PWMG) which can be set into motion when you use the right rituals. The words stir up our Omni-Cosmic psychic forces within. They in turn reach out to the Universal Mind to get the results.

First, you must remove any mental blocks, for you will only short-circuit the psychic electrons as they go to the brain.

Second, get your mental attitude in a positive receptive mood. Pick a special room as your center of operations for your PWMG activity, which we will call your Omni-Cosmic Control Station.

The room I use is painted in a restful shade of periwinkle blue, for me the most receptive color for meditation. It helps to activate the Omni-Cosmic psychic forces. It also gives me a feeling of being at peace with myself. Be sure to use a color for your room that makes you feel content and serene.

Sit in a relaxed state for about 15 minutes and say the following ritual over five times. In a short time you will start to feel the Omni-Cosmic psychic forces working. Do this twice daily.

RITUAL TO ACTIVATE YOUR PSYCHIC WEALTH MIRACLE GENERATOR

Ah-Pea-Ah-Chay-Ray and *Ree-Ten-Oo-Toe,* I invoke the powers of the universal realm to generate my commands for wealth.

I wish to increase the money supply; I know that I can obtain all the wealth, for the Omni-Cosmic psychic forces control all the abundance of the Universe. They will materialize money immediately. It is done in the names of Mo-Toe and Soo-Bee-Toe. So let it be.

Many times when I have done this ritual I will see lovely colors of gold that will swim and curve around the room. This is one of the colors I see, for money is Gold. Many times I will see this in a person's aura.

The right words create the power that sets the PWMG in motion. There is so much wealth in the universe that all you have to do is to reach out and it will come.

This is putting psychic energy in action and it becomes a reality.

ANYONE CAN START THE MONEY FLOW

Remember that your power to magnetize money does not depend on coming from a wealthy family nor does it depend on a college education.

Men like John D. Rockefeller, Howard Hughes, Aristotle Onassis, Paul Getty and other wealthy men of our day did not have great academic records, but they tapped their PWMG and produced great wealth out of the universe.

Desire is very necessary. It will activate your mind and send out stronger currents to your psychic electrons which will tap the money flow to find the treasures of the world.

There is limitless wealth all around us.

Jerry M. gets money from worthless land

Jerry M., a friend of mine, badly needed $10,000 for his business. It was sink-or-swim if he could not come up with the money he needed in a month's time.

In desperation he came to ask my help. I told him to use my Money Magnetism Ritual so he could stir up the money from the Universal Source and get what he needed to save his business.

I told him to say this ritual daily for a month and a door would open for him.

MONEY MAGNETISM RITUAL

"Ree-Ten-Oo-Toe"—say this three times before saying the rest of the ritual to activate the Omni-Cosmic forces in the universe for money.

"I believe in myself and that the Omni-Cosmic Universal Powers within my mind can call upon this power source to magnetize money so that I can have all I want. We are all one Power and I know, I can, and I will, have it through the Universal Omni-Cosmic Power forces flowing through me today."

Eighteen days later a man came to see Jerry and asked about some property he owned in the Helderberg Mountains near his home in Albany, N.Y. Jerry had not remembered the land which he had bought several years ago. As far as he was concerned it was worthless.

Jerry was offered $10,000 by a man who represented a local company in the area. He accepted the offer, of course. He realized that his mind had directed the energy flow to send him the money he needed.

You will be able to produce money from "out of thin air" as Jerry did if you tap your mental power the way he did.

You can materialize anything you want in life if you keep your mind in tune with universal powers and your belief strong.

Tap the source and away you go in a new world of money and power.

Cash appears out of nowhere

Mary A. needed money for her taxes. She was worried for she was on a limited income due to her recent retirement. She came to me for a consultation. I felt she should use my Money Visualization Ritual, which she agreed to do for a few weeks.

Every morning upon arising and every evening before retiring she was to visualize a check in her hand for $500.00, which was the amount she needed to pay the taxes.

This was the ritual she was to say also:

MONEY VISUALIZATION RITUAL

Ree-Ten-Oo-Toe—I direct the Universal Mind to find the needed money to clear up my taxes. I know I can magnetize the money. It is available for me from the universal source. So mote it be."

Within four weeks she saw a lottery ticket lying in the street near her house. At first she thought someone had thrown it away and that it was worthless. A voice within her told her to check the numbers on the ticket which she did immediately. She found it was worth just the amount she needed, $500.00.

What Mary had done was to stir up her Omni-Cosmic psychic energy power and it reached out into the universe, directing her to the money she needed.

All you have to do is set the Omni-Cosmic psychic electrons into action and you will get a response within a short time.

GIVE SOME OF YOUR MONEY TO HELP HUMANITY

Think of all the money you have now. Give some of it back to charity or to your fellow man. This keeps the flow of money going and helps all concerned.

Be generous; donate some of it to orphans in your community.

Think of how good you will feel.

Give some of it to a non-profit organization to help improve your community and make life more pleasant for many people.

You have now directed the money flow along many lines and this will attract the proper magnetic field in order to let the natural law of money increase its energy in nature.

As you attract the right magnetic field, money will flow to you in abundance. Money has to fulfill its natural purpose.

Money is neither good nor evil. It is only an energy that has a relationship to mankind. Learn to use it. Give it wisely to others around you.

Money should be an energy force with which you can do something creative, to aid your race and nation, and in time you will leave an impression of your personality forever.

Money is a symbol that shows the creative energy force within man, which is the Universal Mind that will give him all the happiness he may want in life.

You can charge your PWMG to get all the good things of life.

Betty gets the car of her dreams

Betty J. had always wanted to own a Cadillac. She wanted a blue car with all the extras. It seemed to be only a dream, for Betty was making a very limited salary.

She came to see me for a consultation. I felt she could have the car of her dreams through her PWMG with Omni-Cosmic Psychic Visualization Ritual.

I told her to cut out a picture of the car she had always wanted and hang it in her apartment so she could look at it several times a day. She was to believe it was hers and that it would be available just as if she had placed an order with the Cadillac Corp.

She was to say this ritual after she did her visualization.

MONEY RITUAL VISUALIZATION

Ree-Ten-Oo-Toe, — I direct the Universal Mind to reach into the universe and find this car for me. I know it is available and that it can be mine.

I summon the powerful guide, Ramha, who is in charge of all modes of transportation on the other side and who will direct my mind to get this car for me. I will magnetize the car and have the necessary money to pay for it. I give thanks for all the riches I will receive. So mote it be."

Within six weeks her uncle called her and said a friend of his was selling a blue Cadillac. The friend's wife had died suddenly and she had wanted him to find a person who knew and loved her to own the car.

Betty fit the bill. She had spent many hours with the lady. They had established a very good rapport with each other.

Betty was able to buy the car for a very low price. Her fondest dream was fulfilled. She had learned to turn on her Omni-Cosmic Psychic Wealth Miracle Generator and get results.

You can do this also.

Overaged executive finds a better position

Jerome R. had been a very successful executive, but when he was 57 his company went bankrupt. He was suddenly out of work. It is not easy for a man of that age to find work, especially one that would pay him $32,000 per year.

Jerome was out of work for a year. He was depressed when he came to see me for help. I felt he could and would find work. He had to get his PWMG going. He would not have trouble even though the employment agencies had not gotten him one within the year.

He said, "I am desperate, I will do anything. Tell me what to do."

I told him to spend 15 minutes a day saying the following ritual and sit in meditation to feel the Omni-Cosmic psychic forces working for him.

JOB-FINDING RITUAL

"Ree-Ten-Oo-Toe" — **Say this 5 times before you say the rest of the ritual to activate the Omni-Cosmic psychic forces around you.**

I summon the spirit guide, Tarama, who is in charge of employment and who will help me in my search for another executive position. I know there is a job out in

Tapping Your Omni-Cosmic Wealth Generator 43

the universe for me. I know my Infinite Mind can and will direct me to it. I know I will prosper. I know all my financial affairs will be blessed with abundance and love."

Within two weeks Jerome was contacted by a company he had done business with when he was employed. He was asked if he would consider a job because they knew of his capabilities through previous business dealings. He, of course, accepted it and was offered a starting salary of $35,000 per year with bonuses.

He could not believe his ears. He has since been very successful in the new job and within three years was promoted to Vice President in the company. He knows the Omni-Cosmic Wealth Generator works.

His success story can be yours with faith and my rituals.

THOUGHTS MEAN ACTION—ACTION MEANS RESULTS

Reprogram your mind to believe the simple statements.

I am happy and successful.

I am self confident and believe in my future success.

I am calm, confident and secure in my undertakings.

I am in control of my life and safe in whatever I do as well as benefiting myself and mankind.

I am strong, healthy and a credit to all those around me and my nation.

If you follow these lines of thought and set them into action by your mind power, you will be the person you want to be.

Paul made a fortune in the stock market

Paul W. speculates continually in the stock market. He consulted me one day for some help in this area. I told him about using the Money Magnetism Ritual for help in selecting the right stock at the right time, for Paul buys and sells stock constantly.

He also began to use PWMG each day before he would look over the stock market report. Stocks would jump out at him psychically from the newspaper print. He knew by this he was getting the answers of what to do.

When I first met Paul he lived in a one-room apartment with just basic essentials. Since he has been using his PWMG and the Money Magnetism Ritual he has made $500,000 in 2½ years. He has purchased a lovely home in his city, and just recently bought a new home in the Bahamas for wintertime.

He has invested a great deal of the money and lives on his income, so he does not have to work at a daily job. He still invests each day in the stock market. He is living like a king and making money all the time.

Paul has learned that money is an energy force which you can tap and use for good. He does this by giving back some to non-profit organizations to help improve his community and other people around him. By giving back some of this natural supply he keeps the energy flow coming to him all the time. He has learned to be rich forever. You can profit in this way too.

Randy made $20,000 on his trip to Las Vegas

Randy H. was going on a charter flight to Las Vegas for a short vacation. He had saved all year to do

Tapping Your Omni-Cosmic Wealth Generator   45

this. He was only a clerk for the state with a grade-three salary. He did not have many of the luxuries he wanted because of his low-paying job. This trip meant a great deal to him.

    He decided to try to tap his PWMG for money that he would win when he was on his vacation. He used the Money Visualization Ritual for one month before he went. Every night, before going to sleep, he said the ritual and would visualize piles of money he had won in front of him.

    Then he went on the trip. He won $20,000 in the five days he was there. He came home and was able to buy a new car, get some new clothes and put some into his saving account for a rainy day. He seemed to have more confidence. He tried for a higher grade with the state and received it. Money seemed to give Randy the reinforcement he needed to believe in himself.

    He did change his life style. His salary has now doubled. He knows he can tap his own Omni-Cosmic Psychic Forces when he needs help.

Tim gets the boat of his dreams

    Tim J., a teacher I know, wanted a 25 ft. sailboat. He could not afford it with his teacher's salary. He dreamed of being out on the water, lying on the deck and tanning in the sunlight.

    Tim and I became friendly because we were both teachers in the same school in the evening division of a local university. He told me of his desire to obtain a sailboat.

    I told him about using his Omni-Cosmic Psychic Wealth Generator to get the boat of his dreams. He used the PWMG for five weeks. One day he saw an ad in his local newspaper for a sailboat. It was for sale to settle an estate. The person who owned the sailboat loved the water and was a wealthy, but eccentric, type. The will stated that if the executor could find someone who really loved the water and would care for the boat, it could be purchased for $100.00.

Tim fit the description. The sailboat just happened to be 25 feet. Tim had his boat within two weeks. It was late spring at the time and he was able to enjoy it immediately.

He was overjoyed to be able to obtain the boat of his dreams so easily.

HOW TO BOOST YOUR OMNI-COSMIC RITUAL TO MAKE IT MORE EFFECTIVE

In order to get the most out of all the rituals in this book there is a need to overcome three negative conditions.

First is frustration. Block it out. Do not let it happen. Cancel it out.

Second is negative thinking. When negative thoughts come change them to positive ones. Reverse your thinking patterns in this area.

Third is to establish a good self-image. See and believe that you are wealthy, successful and a credit to your nation, fellow man, and to your community where you live and work.

You will conquer all your self doubts and become a positive thinker and doer. Success and money are just around the corner for you.

POINTS TO REMEMBER

1. You can have the money you want.
2. The Omni-Cosmic power for wealth lies within you.
3. You will be able to direct your subconscious mind to start the Omni-Cosmic Psychic energy flow to respond to you to draw in all the money you need or desire.

4. Wealthy people are no different from you. They just have found the secret of stirring up the mind to get what they want through the Omni-Cosmic Psychic Wealth Miracle Generator.
5. You are the "Master of your own Fate."
6. The right words will activate your Omni-Cosmic Psychic Wealth Miracle Generator. First remove all the mental blocks. Get your mental attitude in a positive receptive mood. Use the right color for your room to use as your Omni-Cosmic Power Station.
7. Sit for 15 minutes to help the Omni-Cosmic psychic forces get into full motion.
8. Desire is very necessary. It will help activate your mind and start the psychic electrons into motion to get your money flow started.
9. There is limitless wealth around you.
10. Give some of your money back to your fellow man. It helps to keep the flow of money going and helps all concerned.
11. Money is not good or evil. It is just an energy that has a relationship to mankind. Use it wisely. Money should be an energy force in which you do something creative. It will aid your race and nation. In time you will leave an impression of your personality forever.

Chapter 3

How to Use Omni-Cosmic Psychic Power for Instant Healing

Do you want perfect health?

Perfect health is only possible if the Omni-Cosmic Psychic Healing Power within each of us is awakened by the subconscious mind. The right words will set off the action and the healing power will begin to work.

Psychic power created us. It can also heal us of all our mental, emotional and physical problems. We all have this power available.

Omni-Cosmic Healing Power will respond immediately when you tune it in with your Omni-Cosmic Power Channel. The right words start the psychic flow and tune in the channel. Remember your words have power, so be careful what you say or think concerning your health. If you send out negative words, you will receive ill health.

Words, used constantly, are reflections of your mind and these thoughts can affect your physical body in a negative or positive way.

Your Omni-Cosmic Power Channel for healing will reach out to all areas of the body to heal it. Once you get this cosmic energy flow started in a positive way all illness and pain will disappear.

Most disease starts in the person's mind and then manifests itself as being real. It ultimately becomes a reality whereby you can cure an ulcer, asthma, allergy, arthritis, hay fever, high blood pressure, whatever the complaint may be.

Direct your Omni-Cosmic Power Channel in a positive manner and then, and only then, will the Omni-Cosmic Healing take place.

Many people live on the pill kick today. Some people take a pill to give them pep in the morning and some take a pill to slow themselves down at night.

Condition your mind. Let the Omni-Cosmic Healing take control. Immediately the taking of any pill will become just a memory.

STEPS IN HEALING YOUR BODY

The *First Step* to healing is:
Believe you can be healed. Block any negativeness within.

The *Second Step* is:
Realize that your ill health is the result of your past negative thoughts.

The *Third Step* is:
Realize you can ask for the healing power to work through your own mind by your own words. (Rituals)

PUSH YOUR OMNI-COSMIC HEALING BUTTONS FOR INSTANT HEALING

There are seven psychic centers in the body that connect to the brain. These psychic centers are activated by the psychic electrons. Each psychic center has its own Omni-Cosmic Healing Button that directs the energy. We heal ourselves when we send current through these energy sources with a positive command. (See Figure 1.)

The right words will tap this energy flow from the universal source and once you learn to do this you will soon have a steady psychic flow to draw on it.

Soon you will feel your body responding, becoming stronger, healthier and more dynamic.

Stop poisoning your body by your negative thoughts today. Your health will become perfect as you learn to tune the Omni-Cosmic Healing Buttons.

START THE DAY WITH THE PERFECT HEALTH RITUAL

Nam Yo Fara On — I am healthy, happy and in tune with the Universe. I shall start the day with new energy as I command my Omni-Cosmic Psychic Healing Buttons to open my seven psychic centers for perfect healing. I know new thoughts will come to me to make my day perfect. Universal love, peace and wisdom flow through my heart and mind. I will give thanks to the Infinite Attunement I have made today. This is a perfect day and I will find all I seek today in the Wonderful Universe.

I DID IT—SO CAN YOU

I was told, when I was very ill with asthma, that I would have to use a breathing machine three times a day for the rest of my life. My doctor told me that only 1 out of every 100 was ever cured of this disease.

I looked at the doctor in a very determined way and said: "I refuse to accept this and when I come back in four weeks for my next checkup I will never have to use this breathing machine again."

With great determination I brought the machine back to the drug store where I had rented

SEVEN PSYCHIC CENTERS

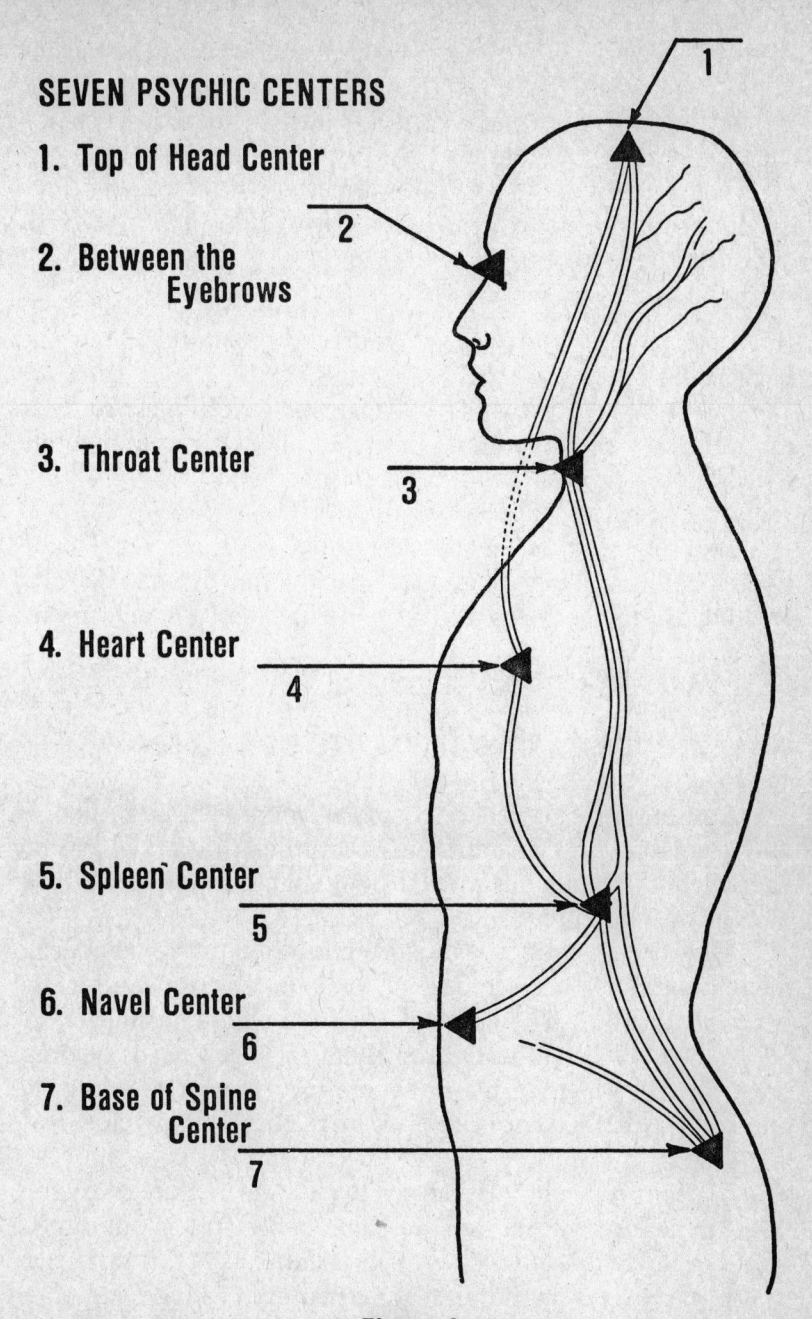

1. Top of Head Center

2. Between the Eyebrows

3. Throat Center

4. Heart Center

5. Spleen Center

6. Navel Center

7. Base of Spine Center

Figure 1

it that day and was in much better health at the next checkup. This was due to my rejection of illness and by sending out a positive thought which tuned in the psychic healing power and in time did cure the asthma.

Reject illness and you will release it from your mind and body. I did it—so can you.

I feel that 85 percent to 90 percent of all illness starts in the mind and then manifests itself in time as a physical condition.

Don't let this happen to you.

Proclaim perfect health by using your Perfect Health Ritual daily which will activate each Omni-Cosmic Psychic Healing Button to recharge the body and prevent illness with the positive words.

COMMAND YOURSELF TO BE HEALED

You have the power to command yourself to be healed by auto-suggestion or concentration. Your mind directs the psychic energy, but without this mental power there would be no psychic or occult power.

One's concentration will aid the healing, but remember no doctor is the sole healer, he is only an instrument for the process of healing. The body takes care of all the healing.

When you have tuned into the area which needs healing, you will feel warm because you are directing extra energy to one spot in the body so it gets an extra charge of psychic healing power.

When you send this energy to the affected area, oxygen, iron, minerals, enzymes or any number of other substances found in the body cells will be rushed immediately to that area.

I offer this as an aid of healing because healing takes place in the subconscious area of the mind and once you do this the healing process takes place.

How to Use Omni-Cosmic Psychic Power For Instant Healing 53

Focus your mind on the Omni-Cosmic Psychic Viewer (See Figure 2) in the following manner:

1. Blank your mind.
2. Fix your eyes constantly on the center white spot of Omni-Cosmic Psychic Viewer.
3. Wish to heal the area of your body that needs it.
4. Use this ritual:

Nama Yo Fara On, – heal and relax this area.

OMNI-COSMIC PSYCHIC VIEWER

Figure 2

Say this 12 times and you will overcharge the psychic energy to aid the healing.

You can expect results sometimes instantly and almost always within a few days.

I offer this as an aid, but get a regular checkup from your medical doctor to see what progress you are making.

Terry's health was restored to normal within two months

Terry J, a dear friend of mine who had been very successful in his career as a research engineer, came to see me one day in a very worried state of mind.

He had just found he had a very serious kidney ailment. His doctor told him this condition would shorten his life and that he needed rest.

I told him not to worry. I immediately felt he could and would be healed, but he had to project the positive thought that the disease did not exist in his body. I told him to repeat the following health ritual three times each day.

Nam Yo Fara On,—I ask Oss-See-Ah, the master guide of health problems, to open up the areas of my mind to help activate my Omni-Cosmic Healing Buttons to free my body of any and all illness or any other negative vibrations. I am happy, healthy, with lots of energy. I feel radiant and attract all this in good constructive thoughts today.

I am free of all illness and negative vibrations. The healing rays flood my whole being. I am healed and perfect.

Terry went back for a checkup in two months and he amazed his doctors for his kidneys were in perfect working condition and no sign of illness existed.

What had happened was that Terry's body had opened up itself to healing by his positive command ritual. When you believe and ask, you will receive.

Terry did it in this case and now he has been healthy ever since. This incident occurred five years ago.

The blind made to see

Alice T, a close friend of mine who had been blind since the age of 12, came to see me one day for a consultation. She became blind immediately after her father's death. He had been blind and she assumed his condition because of guilt.

I said to Alice, "You can see. You have blocked your sight by the guilt you have in your subconscious mind. I feel and know your sight can be restored."

Alice replied, "Oh, I wish you were right." I said, "Reverse your negative thinking today. You feel guilty and this is a manifestation of your guilt. What did you do to your blind father? Think about it.

"Think of your father and tell him you love him and you will heal your eyes so that you can see again."

Each day upon arising and before going to bed Alice said the following ritual to restore her sight.

Oss-See-Ah, —Please direct the subconscious mind to release all my negative thoughts. Set my Omni-Cosmic Psychic Buttons to open so that I may have that which is blocking my sight. I know I can see

and I can again enjoy the beauty of the Universe instead of living in darkness. I release all guilt towards my father whom I dearly love and know he is happy and alive in the spirit realm of life. I know he forgives me too. My sight is perfect. I believe, I believe, I believe.

One morning, after saying this ritual for three months, Alice woke up and started to see forms and some light. Within a week she began to see the glory and beauty of the universe around her. Her sight was restored and she was happy and joyful.

Her powerful words in the ritual released the bondage of her eyesight that she had closed off to herself with negative thinking: she had found the answers through her attunement with her Omni-Cosmic Healing power.

Mary forgave her father and was healed of arthritis

Mary S. had not spoken to her father for 15 years due to a misunderstanding they had over family affairs. Mary had developed crippling arthritis as time went on. She was not able to walk without help.

She came to see me for help and advice. I felt it was the hatred for her father that was causing her crippling arthritis. It was her negative thinking that was actually poisoning her body. I have found many cases of people with crippling arthritis who have a deep-seated hatred for a person or a group. This will cause the dread disease to take over the body. If you cannot love a person, cancel out hate and just send him or her thoughts of help and let it go at that.

I told Mary to call her father and forgive him. She was at a point in her life where she really needed help and was willing to do this, if it would help her health. Mary called her father and cleared up their disagreement of many years.

I told her to use the Omni-Cosmic Psychic Health Ritual twice a day so she could clear her deeper mind of all those negative suggestions she had sent it over the 15 years.

Within six months, Mary's crippling arthritis was healed. She can now lead a normal life. Love, peace and wisdom canceled out the hate Mary had sent to her father. Mary is now a new woman who thinks and lives in a positive manner. She is healthy and has a new outlook on life and people. She learned to use her Omni-Cosmic Psychic Power for better health and happiness.

Susan recovers from pneumonia

Susan was very ill with pneumonia. She had been helped with the antibiotics her doctor had given her, but she could not seem to get her vitality back after three months of being ill. She came to see me for help. I advised her to say the Omni-Cosmic Psychic Health Ritual morning and evening for a month and see how she was at that time.

After two weeks of saying her health ritual Susan could feel her strength coming back. She started to feel like the old Susan everyone had known in the past. She was not used to being ill and lacking in vitality.

In one month to the day she found all kinds of new energy. She went back to see her doctor for a checkup and he found her lungs all cleared up and her breathing normal. She used positive thoughts that were sent to the Universal Mind to help clear her health. They did and she is now healthy and active again.

She had become very negative about many things before she developed the pneumonia. This caused the bad health. Susan knows now that she must keep her mind positive and then her health will remain at a peak level. She has vowed not to let herself go downhill again. She, too, learned how to tap her Omni-Cosmic Psychic Power to maintain and restore perfect health.

Pam overcomes her insomnia

Pam was a depressed, unhappy girl when I met her. She had dark circles around her eyes and did not get more than two hours of sleep a night because of insomnia. Her energy level was low. She could just about get through the day and it was getting worse all the time.

I told her to try the Omni-Cosmic Psychic Health Ritual for I felt it would improve her health, bring her new energy and give her the sleep she so badly needed.

Pam followed my instructions for three weeks. She came back to my office and her dark circles had disappeared and she seemed to have new energy. She said that when she had done the health ritual each night it seemed she was uplifted and transformed to a new person, and it seemed to change her thinking. She felt full of new vitality and in better health, and best of all, she was sleeping seven hours a night compared to two before.

Pam did get rid of some of her deep-seated problems. She is now much happier and full of life. She overcame all the inner fears that had caused the insomnia she had been having for the last three years. Today she looks younger and is full of vigor.

She is so glad she learned to tap into her Omni-Cosmic Psychic forces for it did wonders for her.

Marty's ulcer was healed

Marty J., a factory worker I know, had a bad ulcer. It was getting more painful as time went on. He became so ill that his doctor wanted to operate.

Marty asked me if he should go for the operation which he dreaded. I told him that before he did he should try to reverse some of his negative thinking and in this way he would be able to cure the ulcer through his Omni-Cosmic Psychic Power. He told me he would give this a try before he went to see his doctor again.

Marty did the Omni-Cosmic Psychic Health Ritual for three weeks and started to feel better right away. In six weeks he went back to his doctor to have the ulcer checked. The doctor advised him the ulcer had been healed. It was his mind that healed the ulcer, for Marty had gotten rid of all his negative thoughts and replaced them with positive ideas.

Marty's ulcer was caused by all the stress he had been under for the last year. By saying the health ritual each day, he eased his mind and thus the ulcer disappeared. Positive programming can ease your bodily functions and cure most illnesses. Marty commanded his mind to health. This is what he received. You can do it, too.

BLOCK OUT NEGATIVE WORDS FOREVER

Drop the following words from your vocabulary so that they do not hinder your health or your happiness.

HATE - WORRY - FEAR - SELFISHNESS

Practice everyday to adopt the highest type of thinking and use these words:

LOVE - HONESTY - CHARITY - UNSELFISHNESS
GOODNESS - FORGIVENESS - OPTIMISM

You will charge your psychic electrons to send charges to your body cells that will charge you positively and make you a more healthy individual and a winner in all you do.

Science has discovered that it is our mental outlook that determines how long we live, whether we are healthy or well; or if we are accident-prone.

John's headaches disappear quickly

John T. had migraine headaches for over ten years. He could not find relief from doctors he had consulted.

He came to see me for some help. I told him to use my Omni-Cosmic Psychic Viewer and say the following ritual five times each day.

Nam Yo Fara On — I activate each psychic center by pushing my Omni-Cosmic Psychic Buttons, and send healing rays to clear up all the nervous tension and stress I have within.

I know I am perfect and will not have any problems ahead. I am healed, I am healed, I am healed.

John's headaches disappeared within one week. He had released the tensions that were causing the problems. The headaches did not return (this was three years ago) and he thanks me for showing him how to clear the way, for he had the ability within all the time.

POINTS TO REMEMBER

1. Omni-Cosmic Psychic Power can make your health perfect by awakening your subconscious mind with the right words or rituals to set the healing power to work.
2. Words are reflections of your mind and these thoughts can affect your physical body in a negative or positive way. Be careful what you say or think.
3. You need to believe and to block out all negativeness within and use the right words for healing the body.
4. You can activate your seven psychic centers to direct the healing energy which will respond and make you stronger, healthier and more dynamic.
5. I cured my asthma by rejecting the illness and this released any fear or anxiety that I was holding in my subconscious mind.
6. Command yourself to health with my Omni-Cosmic Psychic Viewer. The results are very rewarding and will be lasting.
7. We are all potential healers when we say the right rituals through Omni-Cosmics.
8. Start today to command perfect health for yourself. Learn to push the Omni-Cosmic Psychic Buttons for healing and increased energy when needed. You will be happier and healthier.

Chapter 4

Tuning in to Omni-Cosmic Psychic Airwaves to Control the Thoughts of Others and Find the Ideal Mate

You can influence and control others with your thoughts if you follow the easy steps in this chapter. You can do this regardless of age, race, religion or national origin. It is possible to work on one person's thoughts or many. This can be done any time day or night, in front of people or in private.

You are the "Master of your Own Future" and you can reshape your life and get those around you to respond the way you want them to. It is safe and it will work at your command.

With this power you can get the lover you want, change the attitude of a troublesome child, get a friend or neighbor to respond to your requests, or get a boss to give you that raise or promotion you feel you deserve. You can influence a person to see it your way or to do things the way you want him to.

Your enemies will become friends and you will be able to control the thoughts of others without saying a word to them in person.

I do ask that you use this power only for good or for reversing negative conditions. Remember, like attracts like so what you send out comes back to you in one way or another. Send out the positive and get the best back for yourself.

You can get people to like you better and you will be happier yourself with this new-found power. You will be that new exciting person whom people will admire and be only too willing to cooperate with.

YOU HAVE HIDDEN POWERS WITHIN

You can tap the Omni-Cosmic Psychic Airwaves that are all around you. You will be able to tune into the thoughts of others and get them to do just what you want by using your Omni-Cosmic Psychic Command Power.

Your mind tunes into the Omni-Cosmic Psychic Airwaves (OCPA). With this power force you can control a person's heartbeat and breathing, stimulate the person's memory process, move his fingers, make him want what you want, repeat words you want him to say and do many other things.

It does work. No one can resist this command power.

I had a student who was failing in all of his subjects due to his lack of interest. I suggested when he was asleep that he would like school and his teachers and that he would strive for higher marks. Within a month the young man's attitude showed a definite change. By the end of the school term he had received all B's on his report card.

We are constantly being influenced by radio, TV, magazines and newspaper ads. It is necessary to know the right words, the right gestures. You, too, can use that hidden power to get what you want in this world.

Thought is a powerful force which we all have within us. It is as real as any material object you may hold. When we intensify our thought waves more vibrations are sent out into the atmosphere. We can reach out into time and space to get the objective.

Every suggested thought wave produces a corresponding psychic response. Look at a friend. Send out a powerful thought. Do it five times in a row. Mentally tell him he is thirsty. He will ask you for a drink of water in a very few minutes. Suggest to another person that he looks sleepy and tired. He will, after receiving your thought waves, feel he is and want to go to bed and rest. If the person believes your suggestion, he will be in a state of auto-suggestion and you can make him do what you want.

USING YOUR OMNI-COSMIC PSYCHIC EYE COMMAND

A powerful way to get a person to respond is using the Omni-Cosmic Psychic Eye Command. With it you can get a person to do your bidding with your eyes.

By developing a concentrated gaze with your eyes you can convince the other person you are correct or you will get him to agree with you.

THIS IS THE TECHNIQUE TO DEVELOP THIS ABILITY

1. Stand in front of a mirror.
2. Stare into your eyes and fix your gaze. Do this until you have achieved a penetrating gaze.
3. Continue doing this until you see yourself in your mind.

If you have an animal, try to stare the animal down. I have a Siamese Cat named Mr. Bub. At first I lost, but after a few tries of my penetrating gaze the cat finally had to look away.

Now try it on a person. Take a bus or train and sit across from a person and send out your Omni-Cosmic Psychic Eye Command. Make him look down, scratch his head, rub his eye or turn his head away from you. When you master this you are ready to use your Omni-Cosmic Psychic Eye Command on the person you want to influence.

Now go into action.

Plan ahead. Think of that action you want to project to the other person before you meet him.

When you encounter the person turn on your Omni-Cosmic Psychic Eye Beams from your eyes to his. Begin to talk to the person in a customary conversation.

Generate a lot of energy. It will break down the other person's resistance. Within a short time the person will begin to agree with your ideas.

USING OMNI-COSMIC PSYCHIC GESTURES TO GET YOUR WAY

Another method is using an Omni-Cosmic Psychic Gesture to persuade the other person to go along with you. You must radiate strong emotion. It should come from deep within, the very center of your being. You will start to get the psychic energy flowing out of you to the other person.

Also, your words should be carefully chosen. Your gesture should be carefully timed so it goes along with your actions and in this way you will be very effective. Late timing will not work.

For example: when you want to get rid of a salesman who has come to your door to sell you something; look very positive and swing your hand to let him know you want him to leave without saying a word.

Whatever gesture you use should be carefully suited to the size and type of person you want to influence. Sometimes you need only use a finger for one person or a hand for a large group.

Timing is the most important factor!!

YOUR MIND IS LIKE A PUSH BUTTON RADIO TRANSMITTER

Did you know your mind is like a push button radio transmitter?

You do not need to buy any special equipment. Thinking will activate your psychic electrons. It will open up the transmitter. Then it will react to your commands.

The process is simple. Your mind activates the psychic currents that direct the energy. Meditation is the key. It will open up the psychic charges and transmit the message.

Try it. Send out the message. It will be received and acted upon.

You want to call a friend that you have not heard from in weeks. Think of that person for ten seconds. You will get a letter or phone call within a short time.

I have done this in my private consultation work. I will see or think of a client in my mind and wonder how he is doing and he will call for an appointment within two or three days.

Remember, when you tune inwardly, your psychic waves transmit your strong mental thoughts which you hold for about ten seconds to get the message across to the other person. Then he receives it and acts upon it as if it was his own idea.

YOU CAN CONTACT THE SUBCONSCIOUS MIND WHEN THE OTHER PERSON SLEEPS

When a person sleeps the subconscious mind is open and will receive any message sent to it. Remember send only positive or constructive thoughts to the other person for you will get back what you send out by the law of cause and effect.

Do not use this power for destructive purposes.

Mary Jane had a son who was complaining about his dislike of the college he was attending and how he was thinking of quitting. She tried my method for two weeks of contacting her son's mind when he was asleep. She flooded his mind on how much he liked college and his professors and how college would be an end for the goals ahead in his life.

Mary Jane's son, one day after two weeks of this programming, announced that he was happy and wanted to continue and felt he had really adjusted to his college career. He did graduate and became a very successful lawyer in time. He was happy he had kept up with his studies and followed them through as his parents had wanted. This happened over five years ago.

THIS IS THE METHOD TO USE FOR CONTACTING THE OTHER PERSON'S MIND WHEN HE SLEEPS

1. Pick a time when the person you want to contact is asleep.
2. Distance means nothing, for this is telepathy.
3. Picture the person you want to contact in your mind.
4. Call the person's full name three times to make contact.
5. For five minutes talk to the person repeating what you want him to be influenced with. *Repeat the same words each night.* Write down what you want to say to him so you will repeat it the same way each night.

You should get results within one week to two months.
I have used this method, and the person being influenced had a change of mind or attitude without knowing why.

Marilyn gets her proposal

Marily K. was in love with Kevin. They had dated for two years. She wanted him to propose for they both were in love. He was a very shy person and could not come out with the words.

Marilyn tried my method of contacting the subconscious mind of Kevin for two weeks suggesting that he propose to her and he did.

Out of the blue one day Kevin asked her to get married. She just wanted him to say the words he really had on his mind to say anyway.

Remember, use this technique in a constructive and positive way.

YOUR MIND WILL FIND THE PERFECT MATE FOR YOU

Do you want to find the right mate to share your life?

Most every person has this goal in life. You can tune into the Universal Mind and it will search for one and send this person to you.

Before you go to sleep at night, take five minutes and mentally send yourself the message that you want to meet the right mate who will make you happy and give you the companionship you need.

Then suggest to your inner mind that you know you will be able to send out your Omni-Cosmic Psychic Airwaves so they will tune into the Universal Mind which in turn will work for you. Your Universal Mind will search out for the right mate and somehow set the way for your paths to meet.

Then go to sleep and rest assured that your Omni-Cosmic Psychic Channel will tune in so that it will direct your mind to find that perfect man or woman you want in life—one that will be good for you. Believe and know that your Omni-Cosmic Psychic forces will work this out for you.

Within a matter of days or weeks, in most cases, you will meet this person by chance. You will know that you were directed to get together for you will be right for each other.

Rita gets her dream kitchen using her Omni-Cosmic Psychic Airwaves

Rita J., a student of mine, wanted an all new modern kitchen with Mediterranean cabinets and gold appliances. She would look at all the latest magazines showing kitchen designs.

Rita's husband is a doctor who could well afford a new kitchen, but he always refused to accept the idea when she would bring it up in conversation.

She came to my classes and when I told my students how to get to people's minds when they sleep, she decided to try my suggestion. She was going to condition her husband's mind for her dream kitchen. This was the room where she spent most of her time during the day and she felt she should have it the way she wanted.

After three weeks of this conditioning technique, Rita's husband said to her at the breakfast table that he had been dreaming about a new kitchen with dark cabinets and gold appliances. He said that he felt a new kitchen would improve the house and make it more salable when they did decide to sell it. This is just what Rita had been projecting to him each night as he slept. Rita called a kitchen cabinet dealer that very day and had her new dream kitchen within a month.

Rita found it pays to condition the other person's mind as long as it is for a good purpose for he will digest the suggestions as he sleeps. Eventually it becomes his idea. His conscious mind accepts it. This is the time the person will go ahead and talk about it to the other person.

Martin was able to stop his wife from smoking by tuning into her Omni-Cosmic Psychic Airwaves

Martin's wife Marion was a very heavy smoker. They were my neighbors before I moved to my present home. Marion smoked three packs of non-filter cigarettes each day. Her doctor warned her many times that it was affecting her health. Within a few more years it would be too late to correct. Marion just could not give up the smoking habit for she had tried many times without success.

Martin was worried and confided to me about this problem. I told him the only way to get Marion to stop smoking was to condition her mind with Omni-Cosmic Psychic Airwaves.

He said he would try anything if it would help. He did not want his wife to die young. He knew she would if she continued this bad habit. He tried my conditioning method for three weeks. Then one day, after Marion had come from a shopping trip, she advised him she was giving up smoking because she no longer enjoyed the taste of cigarettes. She told him she was getting severe chest pains, plus having a constant cough. It was also staining her fingers and teeth too much. She stopped smoking that day and has not taken another cigarette since. This was two years ago.

Marion not only conquered the smoking habit completely, but improved her health. Martin reported his success to me. He was so glad he had found a solution to his wife's bad habit.

This is one of the best methods to stop bad habits without upsetting other persons too much. They will change their thinking when programmed. They just want to change for no apparent reason except that it was their own idea. This is half the battle in anything that is addictive.

Connie gets her engagement ring by using her Omni-Cosmic Psychic Airwaves

Connie L., a student of mine, wanted an engagement ring for Christmas. She came to see me for a consultation and wanted to know how to get her boyfriend of three years to get her this gift.

I told her she should condition his mind each night for then he would think it was his own idea and buy her one.

It was just three weeks before Christmas. Connie so wanted to become engaged for the holidays. They had discussed it, but nothing definite had been concluded on the subject.

One week later they were walking by a jewelry store in the business section of the city where Connie lives, and her boyfriend Larry said to her, "Connie I have been thinking of buying you a diamond ring for Christmas and announcing our engagement. Let's go in and pick one out right now."

Connie was surprised her programming had worked so fast on Larry's mind. That day she picked out a lovely 1-carat solitaire diamond ring which she received on Christmas day.

After the holidays Connie announced to the class her success in tuning into her Omni-Cosmic Psychic Airwaves. For the results, she held up, for the class to see, the lovely diamond ring. Connie told me personally, "Ann, this is the diamond I had projected to Larry each night for that one week. I am so happy. Thank you for your help."

This was three years ago. Now Connie is married, has a new home, a baby boy and is very content being a wife and mother. Larry loved her, but needed some help in moving to action on the engagement.

Judy doubles her salary by tuning in to her Omni-Cosmic Psychic Airwaves

Judy K. wanted to be promoted to a new position that she knew was opening up soon in the company she worked for.

She asked my advice on how to get her boss to consider her for the job, for she had the training and knowledge to fill it. All Judy needed was a chance to prove herself in an executive position.

I told her to use her Omni-Cosmic Psychic Airwaves to tap her employer's mind so he would consider her for this job. She did the ritual for four weeks. One day her employer called her into his office to discuss the new job opening. He told her that he had been thinking about her for the job. She was appointed to it. Within a year she doubled her salary.

She is really grateful she learned how to use her Omni-Cosmic Psychic Airwaves to help convince her employer that she was the right one for the job. It will work for you too if you try. Success and money are around the corner for you if you assert your Omni-Cosmic psychic powers.

POINTS TO REMEMBER

1. You are the "Master of your own Future." You can tune into your Omni-Cosmic Psychic Airwaves to get anything you want.
2. You can reverse negative conditions. You do not have to accept them.
3. Omni-Cosmic Psychic Airwaves are all around you. You can tune into these vibrations any time you want to and use them to control others around you.
4. Your thought is a very powerful force. It is as real as any material object you may hold.
5. Use the Omni-Cosmic Psychic Eye Command to get the other person to do your bidding. Project your Omni-Cosmic Psychic Eye Beams from his eyes to yours in a very casual way to hold his attention.
6. You will generate a lot of energy. It will break down the other person's resistance and you will have him under control.

Controlling the Thoughts of Others

7. Omni-Cosmic Psychic Gestures are sent out with a strong emotion which will start the Omni-Cosmic Psychic Energy flowing from you to the other person.
8. Your mind will work just like a push button radio transmitter through your thought process. It will send out the messages. You will then get the response you seek.
9. Contact the other person's mind for helping to improve him in some way or to get a desire that is good for both of you.
10. You can find that perfect mate when you send out the request through your Omni-Cosmic Psychic Airwaves. It will send the motion to the Universal Mind that will seek out and find the person you want and direct him to you.
11. Rita was able to get the kitchen of her dreams because she conditioned her husband's mind. It was for a good purpose. Her husband digested the suggestion as he slept and then gradually accepted it as his own idea.
12. Using your Omni-Cosmic Psychic Airwaves is one of the best methods to stop a bad habit without upsetting other persons too much. They will change their thinking when programmed. After this they just want to change for no apparent reason except that it seems to be the thing to do. This is half the battle in anything that is addictive.
13. Success, love, money, and happiness are just around the corner for you if you turn on your Omni-Cosmic psychic powers and just believe you can do it.

Chapter 5

Using Your Omni-Cosmic Psychometrics for Finding Lost People and Treasure

Everything radiates energy, from people to inanimate objects.

We realize that fingerprints are left on an object when we touch them. Unseen vibrations are left from our bodies on everything we come in contact with. Even frozen matter will radiate its own kind of energy. Therefore, your ring may reveal more about you than your diary. These impressions will be detected by you when you use your Omni-Cosmic Psychometric ability.

We have logic and reasoning which enable us to solve problems and live in today's world. We also have abstract feelings that we call emotion, and thus we react emotionally to objects and other people, many times with puzzlement because we do not know why we feel as we do.

You get vibrations when you meet people, walk into a room, go to a restaurant, ride through the countryside, shake hands and in many other ways.

Finding Lost People and Treasure

Think back about the times you have been introduced to a new person and said to yourself, "I really like that person," or "I really did not feel right about that individual." We send out energy as a fireplace sends out heat.

Omni-Cosmic Psychometrics is the ability to read the character, feelings or influence of a person or an object by using the art of touch. It can be more literally defined as a "Measure of the Soul."

Through Omni-Cosmic Psychometrics you will be able to tap these invisible vibrations of the Cosmos and find its hidden treasures. You tap the vibratory energy given off by the atoms and molecules that are in all things both living and inanimate.

Your higher mind is able to become sensitive enough to pick up these vibrations and find lost objects, missing persons, valuable minerals, precious gems, oil, uranium, underground water and other things beneath the earth's surface.

DEVELOPING YOUR OMNI-COSMIC PSYCHOMETRICS

To develop this ability may take a little practice, but within two to four weeks it can be mastered. You should sit in meditation and project your higher mind inward to bring out your psychic ability.

THIS IS ONE METHOD OF DEVELOPING OMNI-COSMIC PSYCHOMETRICS

1. Hold in your hand an object such as a ring or watch.
2. Close your eyes and relax your whole body. Use your power words "Nam Yo Fara On."
3. Blank your mind. Turn your thoughts inward.
4. Let the first impression come through. It may be a word or a picture which will be flashed on a screen in your mind or you may just get a flash of intuition.

Your *first thought or word in your mind* is the key to the psychic information you are receiving.

For example: a close friend, whom I had not seen or heard from in months, came to pay a visit to my home. She handed me what appeared to be a piece of stone and said, "Ann, I just came back from a trip. Where have I been?"

I held the stone for a few seconds and immediately I saw a pyramid in my mind and replied, "You have just returned from Egypt, for I can see the Great Pyramid of Cheops and this is a piece of stone from it.

She looked at me in astonishment and replied, "Ann you are right on again. Yes, I just got back from Egypt last week and this is a piece of material from that particular pyramid. That is a great hit on target."

Give out what you feel or think. Don't try to be practical and analyze the information received when you are trying to develop Omni-Cosmic Psychometrics. It is really simple and once you get the technique mastered with practice and meditation it will prove rewarding in your everyday life.

Don't push, just relax and let the energy flow.

YOU CAN PICK UP VIBRATIONS FROM YOUR OWN CITY OR TOWN

Another method of developing your Omni-Cosmic Psychometrics is to take a walk to various locations in your own town or city. Every inch of ground has its own vibrational history. Whatever has occurred in the past still vibrates and can be tuned into psychically.

HERE IS THE METHOD TO DEVELOP THIS ABILITY

1. Take a walk to various areas in your city or town.
2. Still your mind as you walk.

3. Say your power words "Nam Yo Fara On." Let your psychic facilities focus on any impressions that may occur in your mind.
4. Write down the details received and check later on your accuracy. You will find you can actually tune into the past, present and future as you develop this ability.

Paul was able to win at the races

Paul J., a friend of mine from Albany, N.Y., has been able to make a great deal of money by using his Omni-Cosmic Psychometrics talent. He became very friendly with a guard at the Saratoga Raceway this season. The guard let him enter the paddock area and look over the horses each day just before the races.

Paul would get a vibration from one or two horses and play them to win. 90 percent of the time he was a winner using his Omni-Cosmic Psychometric ability.

Paul would also get a racing form and place his finger on the list of horses. When he would get a tingling vibration he knew the horse would be a winner that day. He would not play every race; only the ones he received a vibration from, and then he bet on the horse heavily. This proved to be very profitable for him. You, too, can develop this ability with some patience.

HOW TO FIND LOST PEOPLE

The best way to try to do this is to hold an object or an article of clothing that a person has worn just before disappearing. Hold the object in your right hand, blank your mind, say your power words, "Nam Yo Fara On," and jot down any ideas that come forth, which will be the key to where the person is and why he vanished.

Last March I was working on a case of a missing girl from Canada. Her mother had sent me a blouse that she had worn the day she vanished. Immediately, as I held her blouse and tuned into her vibration, I saw she had taken off in the middle of the night with a young man whom I was able to describe. I felt they had gone several miles directly north of her home. Then I saw a lake and suddenly I felt a knife in my chest. I could really feel the steel and it took me a few minutes to pull myself out of this feeling I was experiencing. I knew she had been killed and her body was in the lake.

This information was turned over to the Canadian Police in her area, the lake was dragged, and her body was found near the middle of the lake with a knife in her chest, just as I had felt. The young man fit a description her parents could identify; he was her killer, and was brought to justice. I just followed one psychic lead after another to come up with the facts. This can be developed with practice and patience.

How I found a lost dog

You can find lost pets by handling the collar of the pet or a toy the animal may have played with and loved. In my work in the psychic field I have been able to locate many lost pets in this manner.

Last March a couple asked me to locate their lost terrier Mike who had disappeared on a Sunday afternoon.

Finding Lost People and Treasure

I held the dog's collar, said my power words, "Nam Yo Fara On" and started to see a scene of a wooded area directly behind the couple's house. (This couple lived in Connecticut and I had never seen or been to their house.)

I saw a road that circled around just beyond the wooded area. Then I saw a dirt road to the northeast that forked off the circular road and a house which was about 2 or 3 miles ahead and I sensed an old man and woman lived there. I could see Mike with them. The dog had wandered in and was being cared for by the elderly couple.

The owners of the dog identified the description of the area as being accurate; they followed my psychic impressions and found the dog well and happy to see his owners. All I did was to follow a series of psychic impressions that flashed in my mind as I held the dog's collar.

Remember, use my power words before you start to tune in so you will stir up the psychic forces present to help you tune in more accurately.

YOU CAN TUNE IN TO FIND LOST TREASURE, WATER OR PRECIOUS STONES

In the past, people from the country knew there were individuals who seemed to possess a strange power which would enable them to find water or minerals in the ground. The person would use a divining rod he made by breaking off a small branch of a tree, provided that the branch had two extended twigs which formed a Y-shape, (it is necessary to have a well-shaped Y for the best results).

Some people would use a piece of metal, which was long and thin and it would work like a radio antenna as they walked over the ground. They would pick up vibrations which would cause the wood to turn down or cause the metal to vibrate. When this happened the dowser (the name given the person using the rod) would know there was water or minerals in that area of ground.

You can use this method for finding lost treasure, minerals, or water.

Use the following power ritual and get a dowser's rod either of wood or metal:

Nam Yo Fara On—Pahs-sah-kahl-yah—Spirit of the ground and inner earth vibrations open up my mind to the secrets of the earth below so I may find the treasures I am seeking. I promise to share my findings by helping my fellow man in return for your help. Thank you so much.

Then take your divining rod and walk until you get an answer which will come as a vibration from the metal or having the stick move. Then you will know your Omni-Cosmic Psychometrics is at work for you. It will take a short time to develop this ability. Test yourself by finding a water vein in your house or street to check your accuracy.

Joseph K. finds his own water well

Joseph K. was attending my classes in psychic phenomena. He had been interested in purchasing some land near his home that was selling for a very low price. He knew that if he could find water on it he could develop it and make some money in the future.

He decided with his wife Loretta that they would try to use their psychic ability, so he followed my power ritual for finding water. They walked over this land, which was about 15 acres,

Finding Lost People and Treasure

several times. Finally they found a section where they felt water underneath. Loretta also felt a strange feeling in her feet which definitely felt like water.

Convinced that they were correct, Joseph bought the land for a very small sum of money. They hired a man to drill a well. After several days of digging the well-digger wanted to give up, but Joe felt that one more day would do it. The very next day they started to find wet soil and found a spring of pure water which made the land very valuable and proved to the couple that Omni-Cosmic Psychometrics does work.

POINTS TO REMEMBER

1. All matter radiates energy. You will discover the vibrations from objects as you attune yourself to the psychic rhythm of the universe.
2. Your higher mind will be able to pick up vibrations which will help you find lost objects, missing persons, valuable minerals, precious gems, oil, water and other things beneath the earth's surface.
3. The first word or thought in your mind is the key to the psychic information you receive.
4. Give out what you think or feel. Don't try to be practical and analyze the information received when you are trying to develop your Omni-Cosmic Psychometrics.
5. Learn to pick up the vibrations of the horses at the raceway and be a winner like Paul.
6. Use your power words, "Nam Yo Fara On," before you go ahead with Omni-Cosmic Psychometric ability.

Chapter 6

Enveloping Yourself in an Omni-Cosmic Protecto-Ray to Ward off Anybody or Anything Standing in the Way of Miracles You Deserve

As you continue to pursue the psychic field and develop your Omni-Cosmic psychic powers by using the methods and rituals presented in this book, you will become a more powerful individual and attract the best of the world's offerings to yourself.

You will realize that the more successful you become, you will be heir to jealousy, resentment and psychic assault.

You will learn to protect yourself by learning how to use the Omni-Cosmic Protecto-Ray which will overcome any negative forces that will come within your vibrations.

THE TRUTH ABOUT PSYCHIC ASSAULT

Today we live in an age with many evil forces around us. If you believe that Voodoo, or psychic assault, does not exist in this

Twentieth Century except in the minds of the uneducated African or Island People of the Carribeans, you are incorrect. It does exist in this age of Space Research. *Negative forces do exist and they do work.*

There is both white and black magic at work today. There is more truth than fiction when you hear someone use an expression, "I feel that person is sticking pins in me." Or you may hear, "I feel that individual is looking daggers at me."

We are all open to this exposure just the same way we are exposed to atomic radiation today. Small doses of radiation will not hurt you, but larger amounts will cause sickness, misfortune and sometimes even death.

HOW TO BUILD A THOUGHT WAVE ALARM TO DETECT PSYCHIC ASSAULT

I have been active in the psychic field for more than 15 years and have worked out a psychic protection warning alarm system. The operation of this alarm system is very easy to use once you practice it a few times.

First you should check your aura. The technique is quite simple. Visualize and instruct your mind that you are putting a beam of white light up to five feet around yourself within your circle.

This is the way you turn on your Omni-Cosmic Psychic Radar Beams. Then concentrate for 30 to 40 seconds and make mental notes on how you feel in the circle, checking any psychic impulses you receive. This will show you if there are any negative thought waves around you so you can stop any psychic assault that is near or within your aura.

This keeps you aware and protected at all times.

By using your Omni-Cosmic Radar Beams you can develop this so that it will naturally be tied in with your thought waves and warn you automatically when danger is near. By learning how to turn it on by thinking, you will put a white light around yourself for protection and your mind will flash a warning signal when danger is near. You will be protected at all times.

It is automatic and works like a flashing radar beam.

Janice overcame a psychic assault

Janice was very upset the day she came to see me for a private consultation. She had received damaging letters which were sent unsigned. They were handwritten and she wanted to have me see what I could feel about the person who had sent them.

I immediately described an older woman who Janice knew was very jealous of her. This was due to Janice's rising career in politics in our area.

The woman was sending out negative thought waves, trying to get Janice to quit pushing ahead in her career and she was also wishing that her health would fail. The vibrations were very strong and negative from the letters.

First I told Janice to mail the unsigned letters back to the lady with no return address. The evil woman would know she was found out. Then I gave her instructions on how to turn on her Omni-Cosmic Protecto-Ray which she was to use for one week.

One month later she met the woman who had been sending all those bad vibrations at a Spiritual Frontiers Healing Service. One of the woman's legs was about four inches shorter than the other and she was in a back brace. She was seeking a healing when she saw Janice. She immediately came over to her and asked for forgiveness for all those unsigned nasty letters because she realized she would not receive healing if she did not repent.

Janice told her she would forgive her, but not to do this to anyone again for she would not be so lucky the next time. The woman was healed at the Healing Service and did learn a lesson about sending out psychic assault for it had backfired.

What had happened was that Janice put her Omni-Cosmic Protecto-Ray around herself and all the negative thought waves bounced back at the woman. When you do this you send a charge back that is two or three times greater than what was originally sent.

It is necessary to protect yourself as you climb the ladder of success as Janice did. If you will follow my instructions you will be able to protect yourself at all times.

HOW TO TURN ON YOUR OMNI-COSMIC PROTECTO-RAY

When psychic assault confronts you it becomes necessary to defend yourself in this world with so many evil forces all around. Psychic energies can be misused by an undeveloped mind or by a person who is full of resentment and hate.

The person who sends out the negative charge may use a Voodoo doll, incantations, black magic rituals or may just direct negative psychic energy force mentally.

If you find you are bothered by lack of sleep, excessive nervousness, poor health that does not seem to improve, marital problems, or not getting ahead in your career it could be that someone is sending out negative charges to you.

THIS IS THE TIME TO PROTECT YOURSELF. DIRECT THE NEGATIVE FORCES BACK TO THE SENDER. WHEN YOU REVERSE THE NEGATIVE ENERGY IT WILL BACKFIRE. It can prove to be very harmful.

BEWARE ABOUT USING ANY NEGATIVE POWERS!

METHOD OF TURNING ON YOUR OMNI-COSMIC PROTECTO-RAY

1. Visualize a white light around your physical body. See it around yourself about five inches.
2. Say the following ritual three times a day for one week.

Nam Yo Fara On—Coe-Nah-Me-I-Mah—**Master Guide of the White Planes of the Spirit Realm, protect me and guard my vibrations against all the dark negative forces near me today. I ask you to remove them from my aura and send them back to the person who sent them to me. I refuse to accept any of their negativeness and send them back immediately. Thank you for your help.**

You will feel your vibrations lift, free yourself of all the negative forces around you, and protect yourself whenever you need to.

Lawrence J. reversed the Voodoo curse

Lawrence J., a very successful business man in my area, came to see me for a consultation. He felt that someone was cursing him with some form of Black Magic for everything was going wrong in his personal life. He asked me to tune in and see what advice I could give him.

As I tuned in I felt he was correct about all the evil around him for I saw a man who had knowledge of Voodoo using a doll to hurt him even to the point of death.

I told Lawrence that good would overcome evil if he opened his mind to this, for the Universal Mind would respond to his request for help and he could send all the evil back to its source. The person sending him the evil thoughts and deeds was a jealous employee.

I instructed Lawrence to sit in meditation three times a day and use his Omni-Cosmic Protecto-Ray, and if he continued to say this ritual each day for a week he would surround himself with protection and drive the evil back to his employee. The Protecto-Ray he was using for protection would make him invulnerable and he would be completely insulated from the negative thought forms sent to him by this Voodo curse.

He followed my instructions to put the white light of protection around himself and saying the ritual three times a day. Within a week he felt freed of all the pressures he had been feeling in his personal life.

The employee who had sent all the bad vibrations had a heart attack within 10 days, for all the negative thoughts backfired and when they had no place to go they went back to the source and the Voodoo practitioner actually killed himself with his own thoughts.

Remember, be careful what you send out mentally to the next person for you may suffer instead if the other person knows the Universal Law that you do not have to accept negative thought forms. I would recommend that you put your Omni-Cosmic Protecto-Ray around yourself each day before you take your first cup of coffee in the morning.

Start the day with a feeling of protection and you will be protected all day. Then you can climb up the ladder of success as high as you want and never be bothered with psychic assault again.

Carol repels a Black Magic attack

Carol J., a professor at one of the local colleges where I live, has been teaching for 15 years. She is an understanding person who radiates love in her field.

Last fall I attended one of her lectures because of an interest in the particular course she was teaching. When I saw her she looked terrible. She had grown thinner and had a worn look on her face. She was not the woman I had known a year ago. Her voice was not steady. Her private life was not happy for her husband had been threatening to leave her. Her status in the college had gone down considerably.

Carol found other teachers were avoiding her. Her students were not satisfied with her classes. This had been reported to the college authorities. I felt sorry for Carol. After the class lecture was over, I went over to see what I could do for her.

I tuned in psychically and found a male student, Michael, had been dealing with Black Magic. He had sent a negative charge to her because he had been given a failing grade in one of her classes in the previous semester.

Carol's position was at stake. It had become so serious that it affected her health, her job and her family ties. When I explained what I had picked up psychically Carol knew who the student was who had done this to her.

I told her to use her Omni-Cosmic Protecto-Ray three times a day for a week. She had to send the evil back to the student who sent it out to her in the first place.

Carol did this for one week, using the ritual of protection daily. When I saw her again, a dramatic change had occurred. She radiated new confidence. Her face looked younger and she had a new glow about her. She was cleared of the negative vibrations that had been sent to her.

Michael, the student who had sent out the Black Magic, had a car accident within ten days. It sent him to the hospital for three weeks. While he was in the hospital his apartment had a fire due to faulty electrical wiring. Michael lost all of his possessions.

I do not feel this student will ever try to play around with negative forces again. The price he paid was too dear. Remember

Enveloping Yourself in an Omni-Cosmic Protecto-Ray 89

negative forces can backfire and the reverse negative energy will be two to three times stronger than the charge that is sent out.

Be careful what you send out to another person. If you cannot love a person, picture that individual in your mind, putting a pink light around him. This will help to neutralize any negative thoughts between you and him.

Curtis wins a hopeless court battle

Curtis T., a government employee I know, was about to lose his home, his belongings and the small amount of money that he had saved for his old age.

A greedy person was suing him for damage to his property. Curtis needed help and a witness to help his side of the story. The person suing was out to get whatever money he could out of the lawsuit for he had done this to another person ten years before.

Curtis asked me for help. I told him to use the Omni-Cosmic Protecto-Ray to stop the legal injustice. He used the ritual for three weeks. In that time the person suing him broke his leg when he was hit by a car. He was weakened and in no position to carry on a strong legal battle. The unfair man became uptight feeling that his luck was reversing. He dropped the lawsuit and Curtis came out the winner.

Curtis was relieved to be back on solid ground without a lawsuit hanging over his head. He learned that you can not fool around with negative vibrations for they can bounce back as they did to the man that was causing him all the legal problems.

Patrick gets a raise and a promotion

Patrick M., an old college friend, was in a bind at work. He was unable to get a raise or promotion because of the negative attitude of a supervisor. All of this was unfair, for Patrick did have lots of ability.

Patrick called me on the telephone one day and said, "Ann, what can I do to get ahead in this company I work in? Should I quit or stay? I am held down by Mr. Frederick, the supervisor."

I said, "Stay, I feel you can get that raise you desire and that promotion. I feel Mr. Frederick is sending out all this negativeness because he is hiding something himself. Use the Omni-Cosmic Protecto-Ray everyday and you will be amazed at the good results that will happen to you on your job scene."

Patrick followed my advice. Three weeks later the president of his company called him in his office for a conference. Patrick received a good raise and a promotion. The supervisor was fired because he was found to be dishonest with the company funds.

Mr. Frederick got back what he deserved. Pat knows how to deal with negative people now, he will not be held down again.

POINTS TO REMEMBER

1. Remember as you become more successful, you will be heir to jealousy, resentment and psychic assault.
2. Negative forces, such as Voodoo or Black Magic, do exist today in this modern age of Space Research.
3. Small amounts of negative thought forms will not hurt you, but larger amounts can cause sickness, misfortune and even death.
4. Learn to turn on your Omni-Cosmic Psychic Radar Beams to warn you of a psychic assault. They can work automatically once you master them. They are similar to a flashing radar beam.
5. Remember, negative forces do exist and they do work.
6. Jane learned to use her Omni-Cosmic Protecto-Ray and she sent back the negative vibrations to the one that sent them.

7. When psychic assault confronts you it becomes necessary to defend yourself in this world with so many evil forces all around.
8. Psychic energies can be misused by an undeveloped mind or by a person who is full of resentment and hate.
9. The person who sends out the negative charge may use a Voodoo doll, incantantions, black magic rituals, or may just direct negative psychic energy force mentally.
10. Protect yourself by directing the negative forces back to the sender. When you reverse the negative energy it will backfire with tremendous force.
11. Your Omni-Cosmic Protecto-Ray should be used every day for maximum results and for constant protection.
12. If you cannot love a person, picture that individual in your mind, putting a pink light around him. This will neutralize any negative thoughts between you and him.

Chapter 7

How to Call Your Omni-Cosmic Magic Sage to Be Your Willing Invisible Slave

When you are trying to achieve something you will find that you can get it done more easily when you can call for some help from your Omni-Cosmic Magic Sage (OCMS). This is another powerful source available to you at just your bidding.

It does not take long to find your Magic Sage and let this spirit help you achieve your dreams. This personal spirit guide can reach all the upper planes on the other side to help you. You will be happier and have help at hand when needed.

John R. bought a lottery ticket for $1,000 a week for life

John R., a factory worker, was desperately in need of money for his rent, his car payments and a pile of unpaid bills stacked up on his desk at home.

The man was discontented and unhappy and could see no help in sight for his financial distress.

He said to me, "If I could only get ahead and obtain money for luxuries and payment of my bills."

My advice was to perform the Omni-Cosmic Magic Sage Ritual to get the answers to his questions. I know miracles have happened when people called their Magic Sage to inspire them with answers. Many of my clients report great success with this ritual.

John did exactly what I told him to do. Two months later he bought the winning lottery ticket that pays $1,000 a week for life. His Magic Sage told him what day to buy the ticket and the store to purchase it in.

He was overjoyed. He paid all of his bills, took his family on a long trip, and is building a new house. Now he wants to help his fellow man out in some way too by doing volunteer work with the blind. It is a happy ending to a sad story. It was all possible because he used his Omni-Cosmic Magic Sage Ritual to call his spirit guide for help and it came.

THE POWER WORDS WHICH WILL SUMMON YOUR MAGIC SAGE

It is necessary to use the right words to attract your Magic Sage to you. Say the words in a drawn-out fashion as did the ancients when they summoned their powerful sages in olden days. I discovered this ancient knowledge when reading some old manuscripts of Tibet.

The power words are *Ohn-Kam-Nam-Ohm*. Open your mouth and say them slowly five times in a drawn-out manner. Then take three deep breaths to relax yourself and close your eyes. Say the power words five more times. In a few minutes you will feel spirit action coming towards you. You will feel vibrations all around you.

Then say the following ritual:

"Come forth my Magic Sage. You are most welcome.
"You will help me in my pursuits for you have the power to do so.
Find that which I seek for me.
So let it be."

Then in *a firm voice say* the following *ritual for protection.*

***Ohn-Kam-Nam-Ohm*—I ask that my Magic Sage be good and a positive spirit force who will come forth to help me. I will not accept anyone who is evil for I seek that which is good only.**

Now you have protected yourself and attracted the right Sage to you.

You have expressed the words and sent the thought that your Magic Sage is coming and will help. You have invited him in. There will be a warm feeling around you and then after a few minutes you will feel power fill the room, and now you can ask him to help you and he will respond to your requests.

HOW TO TALK WHEN YOU SUMMON YOUR MAGIC SAGE

When you summon your Magic Sage you should sit in a relaxed position in a comfortable chair and carry on an imaginary conversation with him. Use the Ritual of Protection and imagine that your Magic Sage is sitting across from you. Converse with him just as if you were talking to a counselor discussing your problems.

As an example you would say "Hello" to your Magic Sage and tell him your problems such as: "I am having a problem with my daughter. She is not doing well in school and does not listen to my authority at home. How can I be helped?"

Wait for a minute and the answer will come to you. Listen and get your mental reply from your Magic Sage such as: "My feelings are that your daughter will show improvement within three months. So just relax and try to have patience and help her all you can."

Then say to your Magic Sage, "Thank you for all your help today. I will try to understand and help her all I can." Keep a record of all you receive and then say, "Good-by. You have been a great deal of help and I do appreciate your answer."

Diane found her husband through her Magic Sage

Diane was lonesome and unhappy for she had been unlucky in love and wanted romance and marriage. She did not feel she would find the right mate.

She came to see me for a consultation. I felt she needed to call upon her Magic Sage for help. Her Magic Sage would be able to search out and find the right man for her.

I gave her the OCMS Ritual and told her to go home and start believing that the right man had already arrived for this would help her Magic Sage because all her negativeness would be removed.

Diane performed the OCMS Ritual and her Magic Sage sent her a thought that she should go to a certain lecture, giving her the time and the place where she would meet her perfect mate. She followed my instructions and much to her surprise a man stopped to talk to her after the lecture and asked her out for coffee. They became good friends which led to marriage within six months. He was all she had hoped for.

All you have to do is summon your Magic Sage and ask him to help you and he will respond immediately.

David A. won nine races by listening to his Magic Sage

David A. needed money to go to college in the fall. He had never been lucky at the races, but decided to call his Magic Sage to help finance his college tuition.

He performed my OCMS Ritual before he went to the races and asked his Magic Sage to help him win. His Magic Sage responded by sending him the thought not to go the next day but to go three days later. David accepted the thought sent to him and went on the day he was directed to go.

He had $150.00 to spend that day at the track. He looked at the racing form and actually saw winners in green letters. His Magic Sage went with him and helped David pick out all nine winners for he came home with a total of $1,600.00 which was enought for college that fall.

It seems that day was the one when all the long shots came in. This is why David's Magic Sage had selected it. David was happy and able to start the college of his choice that fall and pursue the career he so badly wanted. David had found the right contact with his Magic Sage and has been grateful for his help. He feels secure because he knows he will come to his rescue in time of need.

Claire's Magic Sage cured her husband's drinking problem

Claire W. was unhappy and ready to leave her husband because of his drinking problem, for he had been an alcoholic for 13 years. He spent most of his free time in a bar near their home. Many times Claire did not have enough food for the children, or money to pay the rent. She was always short of money and behind on the bills. It steadily became worse.

Claire tried to get odd jobs in order to earn extra money at times to keep the bill collectors from taking the house and other things she valued. They sank deeper and deeper into debt all the time. She grew more discontented and unhappy as time went on.

Her husband Jim, was basically a good man except for the drinking problem. Claire did love him. That is why she put up with him for so long. She came to see me for help. She asked me if she should leave him. I said, "No, call on your Magic Sage for he will help you. I feel he will influence Jim's mind which is the solution to this problem of his." She agreed to use the Magic Sage Ritual and to ask this spirit guide of hers for help.

She told me she had used the Magic Sage Ritual and he told her to release the matter of Jim's drinking to him. She said to me, "I do not know what my Magic Sage did, but Jim stopped drinking within five days and he has not had a drink since. He just said he had lost his taste for alcohol."

Jim and Claire made up for lost time. They have paid up the bills and redecorated the house, all within eight months. Now they are on their feet and very happy. They have found a new life together.

It was their Magic Sage that opened new doors to Jim's way of thinking.. This cured the alcoholism that was destroying his marriage.

Gary called upon his Magic Sage to help him get a promotion with more money

Gary J., an employee of a large corporation in my local area was overworked and unhappy for a long time. He was not being paid very well. He was unable to buy the luxuries that would make his life happier. He wanted to go on a vacation badly, but the lack of money prevented this.

He came to see me to find what direction his life was going. I told him to try the Magic Sage Ritual for I felt his Magic Sage would show him the way.

It happened two weeks later. His Magic Sage showed him a mental scene of a vacant desk in another department. The impression was it would be vacated within a few months. His Magic Sage told him to put a bid in for the job as Gary had the qualifications for it. Gary followed all the advice he was given and applied for the job and a transfer to that department. The job opened up in six months and because he had the foresight to seek it out Gary was selected to fill it.

It is good to have a spirit guide who can show you the future and help you find that better job with more money and prestige. Gary found the time to go on that long overdue vacation. He is happy, successful and knows he has help whenever he needs it from his Magic Sage.

Rose sees the winning numbers on her mirror

Rose J., a personal friend of mine, was broke. She needed money to pay her taxes which were now three years in arrears. She was afraid the city would sell her home for taxes and then she would be homeless. Her house was the only thing of any value she had and she had one month to pay the taxes or lose it.

She said to me, "Ann, what shall I do to save my home?" I answered, "Call your Magic Sage for he will help you find the money. I know he has the power to do this for you."

Rose agreed to do the OCMS Ritual for she believed an answer would come to her. Within three days she did get the message which solved her money problems. Her Magic Sage said to her that he would get the money for her within the week. On the third day she heard his voice and it said to her to look at her mirror and play the numbers in the ninth race at Belmont raceway. She looked at the mirror in her bedroom immediately and three numbers appeared 8 - 4 - 6. She followed the instructions and won $3,900.00 which was enought to pay all the back taxes on her house and buy some new clothes she badly needed. This gave her a new lift in life. She was so happy for she was able to get back on her feet financially and look ahead to a brighter future.

When a need arises call your Magic Sage for he will help you. He will search out the solution. Remember, he is always available for you to call upon.

June's Magic Sage helped her to lose 40 pounds

June K. had been overweight for 20 years. In fact, she badly needed to lose 40 pounds. June had tried all kinds of diets in the past and could not keep the pounds off no matter how hard she tried.

When June came to see me at my office she was desperate for her boyfriend would not marry her unless she took off the extra weight. I told June to try the OCMG Ritual. Her Magic Sage would give her the answer that would help her achieve her desired weight.

June said to me, "I will do it. What do I have to do to get his help?" I explained the OCMG Ritual. She did it for a week. One day her Magic Sage gave her the name of a hypnotist who would be able to condition her mind to help her lose the weight. He told her she would lose all the extra pounds within three months if she did this.

June followed his instructions. Not only did she lose the 40 pounds, but she married her boyfriend within six months. She is very happy and wears a size 12 dress which is just right for her height and body build.

She told me later that if she had not received help from her Magic Sage, she would still be single, fat and unhappy. He gave her the confidence and drive to seek out help professionally. She said, "Thank you for your help, Ann and many thanks to my Magic Sage for he did help condition my mind and convinced me I could do it through my own mind." The hypnotist was a catalyst that started the action to help her mind move the fat.

POINTS TO REMEMBER

1. Your Omni-Cosmic Magic Sage is a powerful source which is available with just your bidding.
2. Call your Magic Sage with my ritual and he will give you the answers to your questions through your mind. It will seem as if you are hearing an inner voice speak to you.
3. Say the power words OHN-KAM-NAM-OHM. Open your mouth and say them slowly five times in a drawn-out

manner. Then take three deep breaths and close your eyes and say the power words five more times. In a few minutes you will feel the spirit action coming towards you.
4. After the OCMS Ritual you will feel power fill the room. This is the time to ask questions.
5 Your Magic Sage is willing to help with the most difficult problems for he can see into the future for answers. No problem is too great for him. This personal spirit guide can reach all the upper planes on the other side to help you.
6 Always use the Ritual of Protection so you will protect yourself and attract the right sage to you. Remember there are negative spirits too. You do not want one of them. You will always be safe if you use the Ritual of Protection.
7. I have seen miracles happen when people call their Magic Sage for answers. You can do the same for he will come to your command any time you want him.
8. After you have summoned your Magic Sage carry on an imaginary conversation. Converse with him just as if you were talking to a counselor discussing your problems.
9. State the problem and then wait for a minute, for the answer will come to you. It will come usually as a mental reply from your Magic Sage. When you have received your answer always thank your Magic Sage for any help he gives you. This reinforces your contact with him.
10. Contact your Magic Sage any time you need to solve a problem. He will help change your life for the better. You will get the information you seek. Claire did and she changed her husband's mind about alcohol. Gary did and received a promotion. Rose did and she won money to pay her taxes. June did and she lost all the extra weight that was unhealthy and keeping her from a good marriage. Your Magic Sage is there. Just ask his help and he will respond so quickly. You will wonder what you did before you discovered this powerful spirit force of yours.

Chapter 8

Using Omni-Cosmic Psychometrics to Revitalize the New You for Better Health and Happiness

There has always been a good deal of discussion as to the reasons why illness develops within the individual. I feel a central truth exists pertaining to pain and sickness; it is caused by the stopping of the Omni-Cosmic Psychometric flow in the mind, which in turn influences the body.

It is my purpose to show you how to keep your Omni-Cosmic Psychometric (OCP) flow continuing within the mind and body for the attainment of perfect health, which is a step toward happiness.

I believe that once you restore this OCP flow in the body all sickness is cured and pain will disappear.

I do not claim to be a doctor, therefore I recommend that a physical checkup be performed, then followed after some interval of time by another medical check to establish what the positive health orientation my rituals have accomplished.

I have received an amazing number of letters and telephone calls affirming that the conditioning of the mind in accordance with my rituals has really paid off.

THE SECRET OF OMNI-COSMIC PSYCHOMETRICS FOR HEALTH

While I was researching some ancient Inca manuscripts I found the secret of controlling your OCP body energies. First, you should learn how to ease your bodily tensions.

THIS IS DONE IN THE FOLLOWING WAY:

1. Lie down on the floor with loose-fitting clothing.
2. Concentrate on tensing your whole body from your head down to your toes.
3. Then relax your whole body from your head to your toes. You will feel all the tension leave your body. Relax now for ten minutes, then tense yourself up again and repeat the same procedure. Do this three times each day for a week and you will feel more relaxed than you have ever felt, for all the stress will leave your body and you will start to feel like a new person. You will feel younger and more alive.

Do this any day ou feel stress for it will release all your tensions and problems for the day. This will restore your OCP flow and you will be that new person you wanted to be.

USE YOUR OMNI-COSMIC WAKE-UP PSYCHOMETRICS

This is another secret used in ancient times to wake up and stir your energies. Before arising each day, when you are still lying in bed, stretch each arm and then each leg. You will find that you have all kinds of energy and this will help to start your day a little bit better. Do this every day for the best results.

Samantha managed to overcome her sleeplessness

When I first met Samantha she looked depleted, with dark circles and pouchy bags under her eyes. Her body seemed to drag when she walked into my office that first day. She looked and moved like a woman who was 20 years older than her age.

Samantha had insomnia and would get only two to three hours of sleep each night. She worried about everything; her job, her family, her health and money problems.

She came to see me for a consultation and I told her to try the OCP Ritual for I knew it would relieve her tensions. I saw her two weeks later and the change in her was amazing. Her sleeplessness had disappeared. The bags and circles under her eyes vanished. Her health regularized itself and she looked at least ten years younger than her actual age.

What she had needed was to get rid of her worries and fears and learn to relax, which she did with her OCP Ritual. This will do wonders for you too.

OMNI-COSMIC PSYCHOMETRICS CHANTS FOR HEALTH

Did you know you can restore your health by sound waves? It has been found that sound waves can restore the OCP energy flow if there is a blockage in some part of the body.

Using Omni-Cosmic Psychometrics to Revitalize the New You

This is another secret the ancients knew and used. The High Priests, Witch Doctors and Wizards actually cured people by their Omni-Cosmic psychic chants. In many cases this was possible because the persons being healed had a psychosomatic condition and their minds would let go of it by the vibrations received by the chanting.

In the eastern world the sages use the word "OM" and it is repeated over and over again until it sounds like home. In ancient Egypt they would chant "RA." It is necessary to say the word over and over again. It builds up vibrations all around you. Try it and you will feel powerful sensations all around you which get stronger and stronger as you use the Omni-Cosmic Psychometrics Chants.

Words said in this manner can actually release the energy flow and build up power and vibrations within the individual.

Here are the four Omni-Cosmic Psychometrics Chants for health. Say them slowly when you do not feel good or if something is bothering you. It will lift you up quickly. Say each chant for one minute and speak slowly:

1. OM—OM—OM—OM—OM—OM—OM
   OM—OM—OM—OM—OM—OM—OM

2. RA—RA—RA—RA—RA—RA—RA
   RA—RA—RA—RA—RA—RA—RA

3. KEY—KEY—KEY—KEY—KEY—KEY—KEY
   KEY—KEY—KEY—KEY—KEY—KEY—KEY

4. HOPE—HOPE—HOPE—HOPE—HOPE—HOPE—HOPE
   HOPE—HOPE—HOPE—HOPE—HOPE—HOPE—HOPE

Find the chant you like the best and say it over and over again for five minutes. Then rest for one minute. Keep repeating it over again for another five minutes. Do this until you obtain the greatest success from the repetition of the chant.

Remember to say each word slowly so that you feel the vibrations from the word. This is another way of achieving success and overcoming the problems at hand within a short period of time.

Rita overcame her blemished facial condition

Rita, a young lady of 21, came to see me for a consultation. She was very upset and unhappy for she could not get any dates, nor could she find a job because of her badly blemished complexion brought on by her own highly nervous condition.

She was visibly upset and highly emotional when she came to see me that day in my office. I told her she could clear up her skin if she would use my OCP Chants for Health. I felt her skin would clear up if her tensions were relieved.

Rita followed my suggestions and when I saw her a month later her skin had cleared and she looked radiant. Best of all she had just met a young man and was now dating. Her highly negative emotional state had been changed to one of a positive outlook on life. The chants had relieved the tensions and had made her happier than she had ever been.

Jeffrey overcame his nervous stomach

Jeffrey, a student in one of my psychic classes, complained often of a very nervous stomach. He had to be very careful of what foods he would eat. Jeffrey had gone to several doctors and they had all diagnosed his condition as one of nervousness and tension. He was told by all of the doctors to calm himself.

I told him to use my OCP Chants for Health and he liked No. 1 and No. 3 so I told him to say them on a regular basis until he obtained their calming influence.

Within ten days his stomach condition subsided and now he can eat anything, for he no longer has all those inner tensions he had previously. He has since married and has a new job and his life is working out very well, for he is more positive about the world and his relationship with others.

Nelson overcame his migraine headaches

Nelson had a very hectic job working in a travel agency. People would constantly call him and change their reservations. His nerves were frayed by all the hectic conditions he experienced each week. He smoked excessively and drank endless cups of black coffee.

I told him to try my OCP Health Chants for two weeks. He found his headaches disappeared. The people no longer disturbed him for his inner tensions vanished. He likes his job so well that he has bought his own travel agency and is highly successful in his chosen field.

HOW TO BREAK DOWN NEGATIVE PROGRAMMING THROUGH OMNI-COSMIC PSYCHOMETRICS

You will find it is necessary to break down all the negative programming that you have sent your subconscious mind throughout the years. This is why you have developed illness at times in your life.

RITUAL FOR PROGRAMMING YOUR SUBCONSCIOUS MIND TO CANCEL NEGATIVE THOUGHTS

Oss-See-Ah—**Spirit of health and happiness, fill my subconscious mind with only positive thoughts. Cancel any negative thought patterns that you find there. I know my Infinite Mind will respond to your re-**

quest and help me in my goal for health, happiness and success. I know that I will be able to reach all my goals because my health will be perfect both mentally and physically.

Cancel any negative patterns that I may have of fear, doubt, guilt, resentment. I want this replaced with love, hope, accomplishment, and abundance.

Cancel any negative emotions that I may have that cause colds, germs, infections, arthritis, allergies or any other form of sickness.

Thank you Oss-See-Ah. So mote it be.

How Ronald lowered his high blood pressure through Omni-Cosmic Psychometrics

Ronald W., a man of 45 and a close friend of mine, was very depressed about his health problem. He weighed 255 pounds and had a blood pressure between 200-210. This was extremely dangerous for Ronald could have a stroke easily, and even die. He tried all kinds of diets and drugs, but nothing seemed to work for him.

His weight stayed up and so did the blood pressure. He asked me what to do when he came to see me professionally in my office. I felt he had a great deal of negativeness all around him. His negative thoughts were holding up his weight and blood pressure. He needed to release them in order to get any results.

Ronald's marriage was not good, for his wife, Betty, complained about everything. When he would return from work at night, he would literally eat all night to work off his frustrations. The more he ate, the more Betty nagged away at him. It was not a happy scene.

I told him to try my Ritual for programming the subconscious mind to cancel out negative thoughts. He was also to use my Omni-Cosmic Psychometrics Health Chants. He would say them twice a day, morning and evening.

Within a month Ronald dropped 40 pounds and his blood pressure dropped too. Ronald continued to use the Ritual and the OCP Health Chants and by the next month his weight had dropped another 30 pounds. By now his weight was normal for his height and so was his blood pressure.

Once he got rid of the negative mental blocks in his subconscious mind he lost his tremendous appetite. His marriage improved for Betty saw him as a different man. Betty and Ronald went on a second honeymoon and found they could live a happy life together in perfect health.

It is so simple once you know how to use my OCP Health Chants and ritual for positive programming your subconscious mind. You will be able to correct your health problems and feel like a new person as Ronald did, with a new figure and better health.

POINTS TO REMEMBER

1. Illness develops within the individual when the Omni-Cosmic Psychometric flow slows up in the mind and then in turn influences the body.
2. When you restore the Omni-Cosmic Psychometrics in the body all sickness is cured and pain will disappear.
3. Learn to control your OCP body energies and you will find all stress leave your body and you will feel younger and be more lively.
4. Omni-Cosmic Wake Up Psychometrics is another ancient secret. While lying in bed each morning stretch each arm and leg for all kinds of energy before arising. It helps to start your day a little better.

5. Samantha was able to rid herself of worries and fears when she learned to relax with her OCP Ritual. It will do wonders for you too.
6. Sound waves can restore your OCP energy flow if there is a blockage in some part of the body. Use the OCP Health Chants for better health. They build up vibrations around you and release the energy flow within the individual.
7. In the eastern world the sages used the word "OM." It was repeated over and over again until it sounded like home. In ancient Egypt they would chant "RA." It is necessary to say these words over and over again for this builds up the vibrations all around you.
8. Rita used the OCP Chants for health and she overcame her blemished facial condition. Within a month her skin cleared up. She also became a more positive person with a new outlook on life.
9. Jeffrey overcame his nervous stomach within ten days after using my OCP Health Chant. Now he is able to eat anything for he no longer has all those inner tensions he had previously. He has since married and has a new job. His life is working out well for he is more positive about the world and his relationship with others.
10. Nelson overcame his migraine headaches within two weeks by using the OCP Health Chants. This gave him the courage to stay in the travel business. He was able to buy his own agency and become very successful.
11. Ronald used my OCP Health Chants and Ritual for canceling out negative thoughts and dropped 70 pounds in two months. His blood pressure became normal for it was his weight that was keeping it high. His marriage improved, for his wife saw him as a different man. Ronald felt like a new person with a new figure and better health. All this was possible through Omni-Cosmic Psychometrics. You can do the same if you have health problems.

Chapter 9

Obtaining Miracles of Wealth, Personal Command, and Joy Through Omni-Cosmic Psychic Photography

Omni-Cosmic Psychic Photography is another miracle power that can change your life in a matter of a few weeks or even a few days. You will be able to draw to yourself, wealth, personal command and joy. It works like the magic we find in Aladdin's lamp, for material things that you highly desire can be crystallized through your mental efforts.

With Omni-Cosmic Psychic Photography (OCPP), you project a picture of what you desire upon a screen in your mind. This mental photograph will then go to work at once. It will change your thinking. It is like a power current that turns on and then supplies energy and insight which you will not be aware of on the conscious level. It will work quietly and give you the results you want.

Your mental photograph becomes an everlasting power that will harness all your psychic energies into a meaningful conclusion. This mental photograph, once in your mind's eye, will work unendingly. The ancient Chinese said that one picture is worth a thousand words.

HOW SOON CAN YOU EXPECT RESULTS?

You may ask the question, "When can I expect results with Omni-Cosmic Psychic Photography?" You will receive results quickly. The moment you send your mind the command and send out your mental photograph, a reaction takes place. It may seem indefinite at first, but the more the mind commands, the clearer the answer becomes.

You will actually see outward changes all around you. Your career will show new and better progress and your relationship with others will become better and more meaningful. Your total being will radiate a new power and you will become a total person.

Do not worry about new thoughts for some things just happen that can not be fully explained. Just relax and enjoy this new power. Expect to get out of it what you send it. Know it will happen soon.

You become what you want when you rid yourself of confusion and negativeness. Your OCPP power will go to work quickly and perform all those tasks that will bring you success.

This OCPP secret was known to all leaders in ancient civilizations; men like Jesus, Buddha, Socrates and Plato made use of its powers. Modern men such as Emerson, Thoreau, Ben Franklin, and many others made use of OCPP power in their manuscripts, books and discourses.

YOU CAN ACHIEVE HAPPINESS

If you feel you cannot be happy or content in your life, it may be that your subconscious mind does not believe happiness exists. You can only attain something you believe in. You must anticipate that there are wonderful treasures in this world of ours for you.

Dare to seek in a new direction mentally with OCPP. With new courage you will become aware of the positive things that are out there for you. Set your mind to action to get what you want out of life.

You have to reach out to find happiness. Don't wait until you have to see it to believe. You solve it when you take a chance and reach out for it and find it is there.

Become positive and reach out for that new idea you have had in mind for a long time for it can be attained, but you do have to go after it in your mind first. Negative thoughts only burden you. Get rid of them. Give yourself credit for being successful and happy and you will be.

Grace finds a husband through Omni-Cosmic Psychic Photography

Grace was 36, unmarried and was quite unhappy for she felt no man would ever want her. I told her to change her thinking immediately. She was to start at once to project the type of man she would like to marry on her mental screen. I told her she had to believe and be persistent and do this each day to get the results she wanted, for I felt the man would come to her in a short time. She did just that and within a month she met a man in a restaurant who fit the one she had projected in her mind.

They found they had a lot in common and married within seven months. In fact I stood up for her at her wedding for she felt that I had changed her thinking, and this opened the door to romance and happiness for her.

HOW TO BE SUCCESSFUL WITH OMNI-COSMIC PSYCHIC PHOTOGRAPHY

In order to be successful with OCPP you must have great desire to want to change something in your life. You should give it a lot of energy and mental thought each day to produce results quickly, for many times there are negative thoughts you will have to erase to get the OCPP power to function properly.

You will have to be persistent and keep flashing your mental picture for you are sending out a mental command and it will tune into the answer and send your desire or wish back to you.

Once you practice OCPP power you will have some new ideas and new understanding, for you will become more positive and you will dissolve negative ideas and feelings that you have implanted within your subconscious mind.

OCPP will enable you to think on a new and higher level and will add a new dimension to your thinking. This will enable you to overcome many untenable ideas.

Don't let inner pressures block you. Correct your mental thinking at once. Open your mind and seek out the results you desire. They will come faster if you put vigor and eagerness into your mental workout. Make the most of each day and live it to the fullest.

When you are depressed, change your thinking immediately. Flash a happy and positive command. All of us have this mental power. Just believe and use it.

Carl received the cash he visualized with OCPP

Carl was upset and needed money desperately. He decided to use his OCPP power after a consultation with me to get the needed funds.

He projected the mental thought that he would be surprised and receive $500 within a week. Within six days a man whom he had not seen in 10 years knocked at his door at home and paid him $500.00. It was money he had borrowed from Carl over ten years ago. In fact, Carl had forgotten about it and never expected to collect it. What had happened was that his OCPP power reached out and contacted the debtor and reminded him mentally of his debt to

Carl and made him pay it. It really works. Just try it and see.

OMNI-COSMIC PSYCHIC PHOTOGRAPHY CAN BREAK OLD HABITS

Omni-Cosmic Psychic Photography can change your life, for you will change your thinking. It will provide you with new mental power. Your mind will no longer be engulfed with fear and anxiety. Positive commands will replace this. OCPP will correct any false impressions you have of your inner being. You will look at yourself in a new and exciting way.

Your mental photos will attract the type of life you want. You will replace old values with new ones. Then you will find peace within yourself and with the universe.

Old habits can be replaced with new ones for they were adopted and were really not a part of you, but something you acquired. OCPP will increase your awareness with the world and work miracles for you.

How I obtained my first TV appearance with Omni-Cosmic Psychic Photography

In 1973, I had a secret desire to appear on local TV. I projected the OCPP method of seeing myself being interviewed by the host of a local TV show. After three weeks of this mental projection a station representative contacted me for an appointment. One word led to another and she asked me if I had ever appeared on TV and I replied, "No, but I am ready."

Within 48 hours she had me scheduled for my first TV appearance. Once this happened the other three local TV stations in my area asked me to be a guest on their stations, within a three month period.

I firmly feel it was my OCPP power that led me to a successful career as a TV and Radio personality and promoted my psychic career locally as well as nationally. For within the year I had a guest appearance on a national TV program too.

START THE DAY WITH A HAPPY AND PEACEFUL MENTAL PICTURE

In order to insure a good day, start it with a happy mental picture of success, love and joy. This will start your mental processes focusing in the right direction. You will look forward to each day as a happy and joyful experience.

When you start a day with a negative mental projection you only attract disharmony to yourself all day. What you think and project on your mental screen is what happens to you. Erase all negativeness and live each day with joy and expectancy that all good things will come into your life.

Peggy gets her dreamed vacation with Omni-Cosmic Psychic Photography

Peggy had always wanted to go to Hawaii for somehow she felt she had lived there before in a past life. Money had been scarce for the last five years and it seemed an impossible dream. When she came to see me at my office I suggested that she should use her OCPP to get what she wanted. She was to project a scene of Hawaii on her mental screen so her mind would search for the answer that would get her there.

Several times a day Peggy would flash a mental photo of herself lying on the beach on the magical isle of Hawaii. She did this for one month. One day she found an old coin on the sidewalk outside her home. It looked old and valuable. A local coin dealer offered her $900.00 for it. Peggy watched the local lost and found column of the newspaper. Nothing appeared about the lost coin so she felt it was sent to her through her OCPP power.

Peggy sold the coin and was able to take the trip of her dreams. She had some money left over for new clothes and spending money for her vacation. She went on a group tour from the local area which was economically priced.

Her mental photo created the situation that led her to find the money for her vacation. Nothing is impossible with OCPP, if you are patient and persist with your mental picture for miracles will start to happen for you. It will be amazing!

Richard gets his dream home

Richard A., a young businessman of 38, had always longed for a certain home. It was an old mansion in his city. It was in a lovely setting near a park with a picturesque view.

The home was owned by the State. It was being used for offices of the State Education Department. Richard had told me many times about his being drawn to this house. He had a feeling he had lived there before, for he had "deja vu" feelings when he walked or drove his car past it.

He asked me if it was possible to acquire this home when he came over to my office one day for a psychic session. I felt he could get it. Richard looked astonished when I told him this. He said to me, "How can I do this? I have some money saved, but the house must be worth well over $100,000."

I replied, "Yes I know this. You will be able to draw this house to you by using Omni-Cosmic Psychic Photography." I told him to project a picture on his mind screen every day and let the cosmic forces in the universe do the rest.

Six months later the State announced they were moving their offices in the Education Department to a new location. The house Richard dreamed of would be auctioned off along with some other state properties within two months. Richard waited patiently until the day of the auction. He went to it with a positive mind believing he would buy his dream home. He was using his OCPP everyday as I had instructed him to do. The house originally was built in 1907 for $40,000. It was worth at least three times the price. Richard bid $30,000 for it and was able to buy it without opposition. It was as if psychic forces did not let anyone get interested in it. Richard's dream home became a reality.

The house was in excellent condition. The State-owned property was always kept up in repair work. Richard is a photographer. He is able to use the downstairs portion for his business and live on the two upper floors. Everything worked out for him because he tapped into his OCPP power source.

It works. Try it yourself!

POINTS TO REMEMBER

1. Omni-Cosmic Psychic Photography is another miracle power that will change your life in a matter of a few weeks or even a few days. You will be able to draw to yourself, wealth, personal command and joy.
2. With Omni-Cosmic Psychic Photography you project a picture of what you desire upon a screen in your mind and your mental photography goes to work for you at once.
3. It is like a power current that turns on within, which will supply energy and insight. You will not be aware of it on a conscious level. It works quietly and will give you the results you want.

4. Your mental photography becomes an everlasting power that will harness all your psychic energies into a meaningful conclusion. This mental photograph, once in your mind's eye, will work unendingly. The ancient Chinese said that one picture is worth a thousand words.
5. You can expect results quickly with your OCPP. It may seem indefinite at first, but the more the mind commands, the clearer the answer becomes.
6. You will radiate new power and become a total person with OCPP. Expect to get out of it what you send. Know it will happen soon!
7. You have to seek out happiness. Don't wait until you have to see it to believe. Grace believed and was persistent and found the right mate with her OCPP power.
8. As you continue to use OCPP power you will have new ideas and new understanding, for you will become more positive and you will dissolve negative ideas and feelings that you have implanted within your subconscious mind.
9. OCPP will enable you to think on a new and higher level and will add a new dimension to your thinking. This will enable you to overcome many untenable ideas.
10. Don't let inner pressures block you. Correct your mental thinking at once. Open your mind and seek out the results you desire.
11. There will be a new dimension to your thinking. Make the most of each day and live life to its fullest with new luck and happiness. Nothing is impossible with OCPP. If you are patient and persist with your mental pictures, miracles will happen for you. This you will find are Omni-Cosmic Self Realizers. Try it. It works.

Chapter 10

Using Your Omni-Cosmic Psychic Rays to Achieve Endless Streams of Wealth

Ralph Waldo Emerson once said, "Man is by constitution expensive and needs to be rich. Man was born to be rich by use of his faculties; by the union of thought with nature."

Whatever you desire you can have. I mean anything.

It can be obtained easily and quickly.

You may want a new car, a new home, a swimming pool, a mink coat, a diamond ring, an exclusive apartment, a fabulous vacation, some money to clear up your debts or an income for life say of $20,000, $50,000, or even $100,000.

Tapping your Omni-Cosmic Psychic Rays is the answer for endless streams of wealth.

YOU CAN BECOME AS WEALTHY AS YOU WISH

One of the first steps to becoming wealthy is the *belief* that you can accomplish this. Next is the *desire* to achieve your goal.

The mind must generate these ideas to accelerate the psychic electrons in the brain to action. When the psychic currents are in harmony with the thought process, ideas come forth that will lead you to a path that will open doors for you. Your Omni-Cosmic Psychic Rays will search out for you and find the wealth you desire.

The Omni-Cosmic Psychic Power is within you. All you have to do is think about it. There are all kinds of opportunities around you just for the taking. Every breath you take generates energy. Your Omni-Cosmic Psychic Rays will direct your mind to find the money you want and need for true happiness. You can live like a king and never want again.

William James, the great American psychologist said, "The greatest discovery of my generation is that human beings can alter their lives by altering their attitudes of mind." Ancient scholars and rulers knew this. Modern man is just realizing this truth again.

Your thoughts will bring you action. There should not be any problem in achieving your direction in life. Remember your mind must go in the right direction first and then you will start the money flow.

Look back into the past and you will find men of wealth, such as Howard Hughes, J.P. Morgan and John D. Rockefeller, made vast fortunes in their lifetimes. They had the belief in themselves and the desire for wealth. These men never stopped going until they had reached their desired goals. Even with high taxes and inflation there are thousands of new millionaires each year in this country. This is all due to their desire for wealth.

You can have that King Midas touch too. Everything that King Midas touched turned into solid gold. You will be given the magic ritual that will do the same for you.

Go to it. Right now.

HOW TO TURN ON YOUR OMNI-COSMIC PSYCHIC RAYS FOR WEALTH

It is very easy to turn on your Omni-Cosmic Psychic Rays. It is necessary to meditate each day for ten minutes. This turns on your Omni-Cosmic Energy Button within.

The first step is to visualize a white aura around yourself. This has been described in Chapter 6. It will protect your vibrations and is a very necessary technique before any psychic meditation.

It is best to meditate sitting on a green rug or in a green chair. I feel that when you are surrounded by the money color it helps to bring it to you.

The right color will set your Omni-Cosmic Psychic Rays out to get the money you want. Meditation for this time period, along with your belief and desire, will activate your psychic machinery to action.

Send the message to your mind and draw the blueprints for a certain amount of money. This will start the psychic machinery within the mind to direct what lines of action are needed to get it for you.

Then for another ten minutes picture mentally what you feel you will do with the money, for it will strengthen the positive electrons and block out any negative ones, if they are still lodged in the mind. This will also generate more energy to give your Omni-Cosmic Psychic Rays more power.

It could come in the form of a check or a new money-making idea. It will be like a miracle unfolding in front of you.

Belief and desire will lead you to a road of wealth.

Watch for results to happen for they will.

Wealth will grow for you like a seed you have planted in rich earth. Your harvest will be rich and abundant. You should remember that it must be planted first for then it will grow. Prosperity comes to you when your subconscious mind believes it will.

As the great Master said so many years ago, "Whatsoever a man soweth; that shall he also reap." Your positive commands produce the wealth you so desire.

Now is the time to go to it.

Start the money flow for yourself today.

The rewards are well worth the time spent on this.

Katherine needed money desperately for taxes

Katherine H. needed money to pay her taxes which were now almost three years in arrears. She needed $1,500.00 quickly to pay these back taxes or her property would be sold at public auction by the city within the next month. Katherine's life had not been easy and all she had was an old home she had inherited after her mother died five years before.

Katherine had never married and had been out of work for the last six months. Most of her adult life had been spent in caring for an invalid mother. She had never received any financial aid during all those long years. Her clothes were always purchased from a local thrift shop for she never had any party dresses or went to a dance in her life.

After her mother died, the plant where she had worked for over 20 years closed. Katherine had been unable to find work and was in dire need. She came to my office to see me for help and guidance. I felt something would open up her financially if she would use her Omni-Cosmic Psychic Rays. Somehow she would get some money quickly.

She followed my instructions and within a week a door opened. Katherine meditated and turned on her Omni-Cosmic Psychic Rays and used the following ritual each day:

Mo-Toe and So-Toe—**Spirits of wealth and abundance help me today. Influence my higher mind to open the necessary channels to direct me to money for all my needs. I know my Omni-Cosmic Psychic Rays will search out for the answer with your help. Get all my psychic machinery working for me so my higher mind** will send all the money that I need. I believe this is possible. Show me the way. Open my mind to those areas that will help me in my search for money. I believe, I believe, I believe. Thank you, Mo-Toe and So-Toe for your help this day. So let it be."

Within a week she saw an ad in her local newspaper. A man was searching for a certain type of antique furniture. This fit one of her mother's old chests. Katherine found it to be valuable and decided to sell it. She then checked all of her old furniture and found many items to be of great value.

Katherine sold the items and collected $8,500.00. She was able to pay off the taxes and her tax to Uncle Sam. She had over $6,000.00 left which was a sizable amount to her. She opened a saving account which was something she had never before possessed. Now she is earning interest and has some financial security. This was all a first for her.

It has brought her happiness knowing that she can afford a luxury at times when she needs it. She did get a job which pays better than the last one. She is a new person today. This is just one example of what Omni-Cosmic Psychic Rays can do for a person when you ask for help!

Marion became a successful businesswoman through her Omni-Cosmic Psychic Rays

Marion J. was widowed and had only a part-time job. She had received only a small insurance policy from her husband's death. She came to see me for a consultation and wanted to know what was ahead and how she could make a living for herself.

I told her to visualize her need and ask her mind to send out her Omni-Cosmic Psychic Rays to find a business for herself. A week later Janice, her cousin, was having a dinner party. She asked Marion about a caterer. Marion was also invited to this party and she found that the food could have been served and prepared differently to be more pleasing to the guests. She remembered that at her own dinner parties her guests had always raved about her appetizers. Now it came to her!

This was the business she was to go into. She started working in her modest kitchen. She had some business cards printed and advertised in her local newspaper. Within a few days her telephone was ringing with people who needed her catering services. Within a short time Marion was able to hire a helper and within four months she was taking in more money than she had ever dreamed possible.

You can use your mind to answer your dreams or desires by sending out our Omni-Cosmic Psychic Rays that will work wonders for you just as they did for Marion who is constantly busy and does not have any financial worries today.

Marion has money in the bank today. She has several employees working for her now as well as a long list of satisfied customers who call her for her catering services each time they give a party.

She is averaging about $20,000 a year for herself after bills are paid.

Success and money were hers by asking her Omni-Cosmic Psychic Rays that are available to all. Try it and you will see how fast it will work for you.

How Fred tapped his Omni-Cosmic Psychic Rays and became wealthy

Fred J., a student of mine in one of my psychic classes, wanted to achieve financial independence.

He had been an average student with only a high school education, but had a strong desire to achieve security. He also had the dream that with money he would help humanity in some way.

All of Fred's motives were excellent. He worked as a clerk in a stationery store and his environment did not offer any sudden road to wealth. He was very involved with his psychic growth and had the desire and belief that he would become very wealthy in the future. This is half the battle. He believed in himself.

He used his Omni-Cosmic Psychic Rays (OCPR) daily. He visualized an endless stream of money coming to him from the universal storehouse which is always full and abundant. The supply of riches is there just waiting to be tapped.

Within two months after using his Omni-Cosmic Psychic Rays he received a letter from a lawyer in Los Angeles. It stated that he had received an inheritance of $60,000 from an aunt whom he had not seen in over twenty years.

This was totally unexpected ... a miracle.

Fred knew he had the capital at this point to invest in the stock market so he could make his fortune and have financial security. He came to see me for a consultation. I told him he had developed a great deal of psychic ability in my classes. I felt he should pursue investing in the stock market. He was to go by his feelings. It is the psychic operating on you when you don't think about it ... it just flashes in suddenly.

It could be a thought, a feeling or a vision. All of this is psychic . . . .

Fred had this definite goal in mind. He would sit in a comfortable chair and turn on his OCPR each day for the proper guidance to choose the right stock investment.

Fred did buy the stocks through his psychic feelings. Within two years he had $500,000 in the bank.

He is still investing. He has money in the bank, and takes vacations twice a year. He is happy because he found the road to success and wealth through his meditation and use of his Omni-Cosmic Psychic Rays.

$100,000 comes to Florence out of the blue

Florence, a woman in her forties, always attended my lectures when I gave them in my local area. She had been short of money for years. I mean, really poor. She had been on welfare for ten years. Her shabby clothes came from friends or the Salvation Army. She had never been able to buy anything new for herself in many years.

In one of my lectures I was speaking about how to tap your Omni-Cosmic Psychic Rays to find money in the universe.

After the lecture Florence said to me, "I do not feel this is possible for me to do. There is not any money due me in any way. I do not have any rich relatives who could leave me an inheritance. I do not have any creative ideas that would make me a fortune. Will this work for me?"

I told her, "Yes, think positive and cancel out your negative programming immediately. Begin to project the idea that money will come to you. You will direct the Omni-Cosmic forces to search out for money and it will come to you.

"Believe and expect money will come.

"You will be surprised when it comes through an unexpected source."

She agreed to do this. She had nothing to lose but time. Florence had plenty of this for she was a housewife with grown children.

Florence did this for six weeks. One day her brother had some Irish Sweepstake tickets for sale. She decided to buy one for the fun of it.

A miracle happened to Florence.
She won $100,000 when they had the drawing.
Money did come from an unexpected source just the way I felt it would.

USE OMNI-COSMIC CABLEGRAMS FOR LUCK AND SUCCESS

Your subconscious mind needs to get a flow of ideas that will stir up the energy which in turn starts the Omni-Cosmic Psychic Rays to action. It is a good move on your part to send it some positive Omni-Cosmic Cablegrams every morning before you start the day. Say each cablegram over five times out loud to get the maximum results. This will stir up your psychic energy sources for greater action.

I am healthy.
I am happy and successful.
I am rich and magnetize money to me easily.
I am wealthy.
I desire $10,000. (State an amount of money you want immediately.)

These Omni-Cosmic Cablegrams will fill your subconscious mind with positive action to search it out for you. Your higher mind will lead your consciousness to find it. You will be directed to the right person who can get you the money, success or whatever you need in life. You may be directed to be in a certain place at the right time to be lucky. Timing is very important for success. Prepare your future with your Omni-Cosmic Cablegrams.

POINTS TO REMEMBER

1. Whatever you desire can be obtained by tapping your Omni-Cosmic Psychic Rays.

2. One of the first steps to becoming wealthy is the *belief* that you can accomplish this. Next is the *desire* to achieve your goal.
3. The mind will generate your ideas to accelerate the psychic electrons in the brain to action.
4. When the psychic currents are in harmony with the thought process, ideas come forth that will lead you to a path that will open doors for you.
5. Your Omni-Cosmic Psychic Rays will search out for and find the money you desire.
6. Thoughts bring action. Your mind must go in the right direction first and then you will start the money flow.
7. Visualize a white aura around yourself before going into any psychic meditation. It is best to meditate sitting on a green rug or green chair for when you are surrounded by the money color it helps bring it to you.
8. Draw the blueprints in your mind for a certain amount of money. This will start the psychic machinery within the mind to direct what lines of action are needed to get it for you.
9. Wealth will grow for you like a seed you have planted in rich earth. Your harvest will be rich and abundant. Remember that it must be planted first; then it will grow. Prosperity comes to you when your subconscious mind believes it will.
10. Omni-Cosmic Cablegrams will fill your subconscious mind with positive action to search out your desire. Your higher mind will lead your consciousness to find it.
11. You will be directed to the right person who can get you the money, success or whatever you need in life.
12. You will be directed to be in a certain place at the right time to be lucky. Timing is very important for success.
13. You will be surprised and happy to see the miracles that happen when you use your Omni-Cosmic Psychic Rays for a short time. Whatever you desire you will have!

Chapter 11

How Omni-Cosmic Psychometrics Can Reveal Miraculous Instant Answers in Dreams and Visions

Dreams and visions have been discussed since the beginning of time. In the ancient world, dreams were prophecies of things to come, both good and bad omens sent from the gods.

It was not until the 1900's that dreams were explored on a scientific level. Dr. Sigmund Freud opened new doors to psychoanalysis when he explored the value of dreams in terms of therapy for patients who had emotional disturbances. He believed all dreams were reflections of some sexually repressed wish. Dr. Carl Jung disagreed with Freud's theory and believed that people received hidden messages that he called "Collective Unconscious" from their subconscious minds when dreaming.

We live in an outer world that uses our conscious mind, but there is an inner world of dreams that come through the subconscious mind when we sleep. There is nothing new about dreams; Adam and Eve had their dreams in the Garden of Eden.

All people as well as animals dream. Do you know that you spend one third of your life in the dream state? The mind and world of dreams have always fascinated men and women. Many times we find dreams are of a precognitive nature for they can transcend time and space.

Dreaming is thinking in your sleep. If you live in a confused or unhappy world, you can build a rainbow of happiness through your dreams.

You will be able to change a hopeless situation to one of happiness. Your psychic electrons will attune your being to the higher universal forces and reshape your world. You will get miraculous instant answers through your dreams and visions.

YOUR DREAMS CAN BRING YOU ALL YOU WANT

God created the Universe from a dream He had of Creation. He drew the blueprints in His mind and by turning on His Omni-Cosmic Psychometrics He was able to express it in living form. Your dreams will always come first before you create anything.

The architect's blueprint for your home must exist in someone's mind before you can actually build it. It is the conscious mind that draws up the Omni-Cosmic thought forms that will reshape your destiny. The subconscious mind will program your Omni-Cosmic Psychometrics to bring it to pass.

HOW TO USE YOUR OMNI-COSMIC PSYCHOMETRICS TO MAKE YOUR DREAMS COME TRUE

The first step in reshaping your destiny is to write down on a blank piece of paper what you wish to create in your daily world. List your ideals and talents that you want to bring forth in this everyday world of yours.

This is an example of what you would write:

1. I wish to have an income of $30,000 each year.
2. I wish to meet the right mate and fall in love and marry.
3. I wish to find the right career that suits me best.

4. I wish to find the right answer that will start my life on the road to wealth.
5. I wish to change my home to one more of my liking and one that I can afford.
6. I wish to heal my health problem (list the problem).
7. I wish to develop my writing talent and sell my material.

The next step after you have written your desires is to read them once in the morning before having your breakfast so you will start to program your day correctly. Also read them before you go to sleep for they will work on your subconscious mind. This will in turn reach the universal mind which will set your desires into action within a short time.

As some of the wishes come out, rewrite the wishes until you have all of them accomplished.

Then use the following ritual for programming your Omni-Cosmic Psychometrics to bring forth dreams and visions to you during your sleep state.

"I call on March-ee-ah, spirit of the dream world. Let my subconscious mind send me all my dreams and make them a reality. I know you have the power to do this through my dream state. I know my dreams will come to me quickly and bring me the happiness I need and desire. Thank you March-ee-ah for your help. So let it be."

Omni-Cosmic Psychometrics is the method to energize your inherent psychic energy to bring your ideas projected from your subconscious to a reality.

I used this ritual to find a new house. Within three weeks I saw an ad in the real estate section of the local newspaper for a house in the best neighborhood in Albany for a ridiculously low price. It seemed that the lady who lived there wanted to move to Florida because her husband had died and she felt all alone. The lady's relatives were all in Florida. She sold the house to me for $10,000 below the market price which was just what I could afford at the time. So you can see Omni-Cosmic Psychometrics attracted the right house at the right price to me, and it can do the same for you.

GREAT MEN OF HISTORY USED THEIR OMNI-COSMIC PSYCHOMETRICS TO OBTAIN THEIR DREAMS

It has been said, "To be like Shakespeare, you should think and dream the thoughts that Shakespeare did."

Christopher Columbus dreamed of a new world and found it.

Thomas Edison dreamed of a light bulb and created it.

Abraham Lincoln dreamed of freeing the slaves and bringing the nation together into one union and did it.

Alexander Graham Bell dreamed of transmitting a voice on wire and created the telephone.

George Washington dreamed of winning the Revolutionary War through his visions. He was able to accomplish it and establish a new nation at a time when it looked hopeless.

Jules Verne, an author of the 19th century, dreamed of modern inventions such as television, radio, submarines, ships and airplanes. He was actually seeing ahead to what was to come in the 20th century.

Pablo Picasso, the great modern artist, dreamed of art imagery when he slept which led him to become famous and change his artistic style. He became one of history's highest-paid artists.

If you wish to follow the paths of famous persons who have accomplished certain things, try to study their lives and create their dreams in your own mind. You will then be able to accomplish whatever you seek.

Eileen found her future husband in a dream

Eileen M. had not been very lucky in love. She felt so alone. She wanted to marry desperately when she came to see me for a consultation. I felt that if she used Omni-Cosmic Psychometrics along with my ritual she would meet someone within a month. Eileen did not go out very much or mingle with people. Her life was secluded.

Eileen used my Omni-Cosmic Psychometric Ritual. Three nights later in a dream she saw the man she would meet and marry. She also saw herself going to a particular theatre where this man would sit beside her on the right and start a conversation during the intermission.

Eileen followed her dream and went to the theatre the night a certain play was scheduled that she had seen in her dream. Just the way she had seen it in the dream, a man sat on her right and struck up a conversation. They went out for a drink after the play and he asked her for a date the very next night. After they had compared notes they found that they were both single, lonely and both searching for the right mate for a long time.

Within eight months they married and have been happy ever since. Eileen knew it was her Omni-Cosmic Psychometric ritual that led her to find the right man and the happiness she had always dreamed of, but never believed she would find in her lifetime.

OMNI-COSMIC PSYCHOMETRICS CAN GIVE YOU AN ANSWER WITHIN A SHORT TIME

One of the best ways to tap your subconscious mind for quick answers is to ask yourself for help before you go to sleep. You will be relaxed and confident that your subconscious mind will search out the answers you need the next day.

This is the ritual you should use:

> **March-ee-ah, Spirit of the dream world, direct my mind to seek out the right answers so I may know when I awake the right direction to go. I want to inspire and uplift people that I deal with for I know you will help me tonight to give the right answers tomorrow for my task ahead. Thank you, March-ee-ah, for your help.**

Recite this ritual with belief that an answer will come and your spirit guide will help you find it.

For example: the day before an important lecture I will say the following ritual:

> **I ask March-ee-ah to inspire me so that I will say the right words to inspire the group that I am addressing tomorrow, so that my time is not wasted, nor theirs. Thank you for all your help and guidance March-ee-ah. So let it be.**

I find the next day when it is lecture time my mind is inspired to say the right words and I also find that I do relate to the group successfully so that we all get something out of the time.

You only have to ask for help and it will come quickly when you tap your subconscious through your Omni-Cosmic Psychometrics.

Perry was healed through a dream

Perry had a very bad heart condition and also a serious ulcer. His doctor wanted to remove the ulcer, but was afraid to operate due to the heart condition.

I told Perry to use the Omni-Cosmic Psychometrics ritual and program his dreams for a healing, which he did faithfully for two months.

He used the following ritual:

I ask March-ee-ah, Spirit of the Dream World, for help to heal my body of all its problems so that I may carry on my life in good health. Heal the ulcer so I will not have to have an operation and also heal my heart. Remove all negative thoughts in my subconscious that are causing my ill health. Thank you, March-ee-ah. So let it be.

Perry went back to the doctor in ten weeks and the doctor found his ulcer healed and his heart condition greatly improved. His dream state removed the frustrations that were causing the ulcer and by positive programming he helped the heart condition also.

Chester used his Omni-Cosmic Psychometrics to get the money he needed to save his business

Chester, a friend of mine, was in desperate financial condition with his business. It had been slow and too many creditors were about to force him out of it. He needed $25,000 quickly to save himself from bankruptcy.

I suggested that he use my Omni-Cosmic Psychometrics ritual for a few weeks to help find an answer for his financial worries. Within four weeks, a friend he had not seen in ten years came to see him about going into a business partnership with him. His friend had $25,000 in cash to invest. That was just what Chester needed to save his business. The two formed a partnership and have expanded the business operation, and are very successful today.

Francis wanted to find the right business

Francis J. wanted to own his own business. He did not know just what direction to go. He used my Omni-Cosmic Psychometric dream ritual for an answer.

One night after a week of using the ritual he dreamed of a small pizza shop that was about to be sold due to the owner's ill health. When he awoke Francis realized this was the type of business he had been looking for.

Every day he searched his local newspaper for a business of this type. Within two weeks he saw an ad that fit the dream. He found it was within his reach money-wise. He purchased it immediately.

He was able to learn the business easily and is quite successful. He has bought a new house, a new car and met the girl of his dreams one day in his store when she decided to come in and order a pizza for the office she worked in. Francis has found all that he wanted and is thinking of expanding his business at the present time.

YOU CAN PROGRAM YOUR MIND FOR PSYCHIC ANSWERS

Dreams can be very psychic for you. They will sometimes reveal something about your future. Dreams can also guide you to take a certain course of action in order to complete your destiny in life.

Clairvoyants are able to see a person's past, present and future by psychic seeing. They are able to transcend time and space to accomplish this. Your higher mind knows the answer.

When you program your mind before going to sleep you can actually get a responsive answer to questions you pose it. You can see a preview of your future in this way. Many times you will get symbolic answers that need to be interpreted.

It is best to keep a pad and pencil by your bedside so you will be able to write down and date your dreams each day. In this way you will be able to see what your subconscious mind is trying to tell you when you sleep. You will be able to see how accurate you are psychically and how quickly your dreams work out for you. ESP is easiest to pick up in the dream state for your conscious mind is asleep and the psychic works without interference.

Try writing down your dreams for a month. You will be surprised how much information will be made available to you.

Chris finds a missing paper through a dream

Christopher K., a friend and lawyer whom I see quite often at a local club, had lost a valuable paper which he needed for a trial that was coming up within the following week.

He called me for help. I told him to project the wish to his subconscious mind before he went to sleep for it would direct him to where he put the document. I felt he had misplaced it with other valuable papers in someone else's file.

He did this for three nights using his Omni-Cosmic Psychometrics. On the third night he saw clearly in his dream state the missing paper and also the name of the client's file that he had accidentally placed it in.

He went to the office the next morning, walked over to his file cabinet and pulled out the paper in a matter of minutes. Of course Chris was relieved, but also amazed that it was so easy to tap his deeper mind through Omni-Cosmic Psychometrics.

DREAMS CAN RESHAPE YOUR FUTURE

Your Omni-Cosmic Psychometrics can do a great deal for your future. It is advisable that every evening before you go to sleep, you condition your subconscious mind with a number of pictures and suggestions of some desire you may want to materialize in life. This is actually programming your subconscious mind to make it part of your dreams. In this way it will become a reality. You can reshape your life ahead. You will be able to make yourself become what you want to be.

Picture in your mind the type of person you want to be. Draw a new plan of yourself for your subconscious mind to work on when you sleep. See yourself as a successful actor, lover, businessman, teacher, financier or whatever else appeals to you for your future. It is like casting a role on the stage of life. You act out what you really want to be.

In time your conscious mind will realize it. Then it happens.

It is simple. You need to be motivated, be patient and be persistent.

Your dreams in time become a reality.

My dreams became a reality

In 1965 I first realized my psychic ability. When I became confident about it, I would visualize myself on a stage in front of a large audience or see myself in front of a TV camera. I did this for two months. At the end of this time period a local TV station asked me to appear as a guest. A month later three other stations locally had me do guest appearances. Two of the TV stations asked me to be a regular guest for several months. It seemed that once the suggestion was accepted, my deeper mind, the picture in my mind, became a reality. I did become a well-known personality on TV and radio as well as being on stage doing lectures locally and nationally.

I know it works because I had the proof.

POINTS TO REMEMBER

1. Dreams and visions have been discussed since the beginning of time. In the ancient world, dreams were prophecies of things to come, both good and bad omens sent from the gods.
2. We live in an outer world that uses our conscious mind but there is an inner world of dreams that come through the subconscious mind when we sleep.
3. All people as well as animals dream. You spend one-third of your life in the dream state. Dreams can be of a precognitive nature and can transcend time and space.
4. Dreaming is thinking in your sleep. If you live in a confused or unhappy world, you can build a rainbow of happiness through your dreams.
5. You will be able to change a hopeless situation to one of happiness. Your psychic electrons will attune your being to the higher universal forces and reshape your world. You will get miraculous instant answers through your dreams and visions.
6. It is your conscious mind that draws up the Omni-Cosmic thought forms that will reshape your destiny. The subconscious mind will program your Omni-Cosmic Psychometrics to bring it to pass.
7. Omni-Cosmic Psychometrics is the method to energize your inherent psychic energy to bring your ideas projected from your subconscious to reality.
8. If you wish to follow the paths of famous persons who have accomplished certain things, try to study their lives and create their dreams in your own mind and you will accomplish whatever you seek.
9. Eileen knew it was her Omni-Cosmic Psychometric ritual that led her to find the right man and the happiness she had always dreamed of, but never believed she would find in her lifetime.

Miraculous Instant Answers in Dreams and Visions 141

10. One of the best ways to tap your subconscious mind for answers quickly is to ask yourself for help before you go to sleep. You will be relaxed and confident that your subconscious mind will search out the answers you need the next day.
11. Perry used Omni-Cosmic Psychometrics and healed his ulcer. His dream state removed the frustrations that were causing the ulcer and by positive programming he helped his heart condition too.
12. Chester used my Omni-Cosmic Psychometrics ritual which saved his business. He found a friend from the past to form a partnership with and the two have expanded the business operation and are very successful today.
13. Francis found all he wanted in life; a business, a new home, a new car and a wife, all through Omni-Cosmic Psychometrics.
14. Dreams can guide you to take a certain course of action or to see into the future so you will be able to complete your destiny in life.
15. Try writing down your dreams for a month. You will be surprised how much information will be made available to you.
16. Christopher found a missing legal paper through Omni-Cosmic Psychometrics. He was amazed it was so easy to do.
17. Dreams can reshape your future. Picture the type of person you want to be. Draw a new plan of yourself for your subconscious mind to work on when you sleep. It is like casting a role on the stage of life. You act out what you really want to be. In time your conscious mind will realize it. Then it happens.
18. Your dreams in time will become a reality through Omni-Cosmic Psychometrics.

Chapter 12

Omni-Cosmic Psychometrics Can Materialize Miraculous Riches You Desire Through Using Omni-Cosmic Telegrams

Have you ever wished to find a magical way to achieve a Midas touch?

Have you wanted to know how to tap your power source so you will be able to materialize all the riches you desire?

You can be powerful enough to turn your thoughts into riches for your mental power can bring you all the money and wealth you want by tapping your Omni-Cosmic Psychometrics (OCP).

With OCP power you can successfully trigger your subconscious mind with so much energy that you will be led to your pile of riches. Once you get the money flow going in your direction it will steadily come to you naturally.

I have met many wealthy people in my lifetime. I have found that they all have the same mental attitudes, beliefs and desires. They all knew how to direct their minds by using certain mental thought commands which have led them to money, recognition and success.

Your subconscious mind is aware of everything around you. The key is programming your mind with the right words that represent power and wealth. This starts the action. Your subconscious mind links with the Universal Mind, for all this is a part of the OCP power which is within each of us.

SEVEN OMNI-COSMIC TELEGRAMS THAT WILL START YOUR OCP POWER FUNCTIONING

1. *I Wish—Ree-Ten-Oo-Toe,* **Spirit of Wealth and Abundance, send me the power through my subconscious mind enabling me to release new ideas that will bring me wealth. Thank you, Ree-Ten-Oo-Toe, for your help. So let it be.**

Repeat this Omni-Cosmic Telegram out loud five times and then sit quietly and say it over again five times mentally. It will reach the Universal Mind through the spirit force you call on and stir up your mental machinery to bring it to a reality. The wealth of the universe is all around you. You just have to know how to draw it to you.

REMEMBER, WHAT YOU SEND OUT
YOU WILL GET BACK IN TIME—
SEE YOUR WISH AS ALREADY FULFILLED

Mentally see yourself receiving new and marvelous ideas that will make you wealthy. See money coming in from many sources. Visualize yourself going on a spending spree with a handful of $100.00 bills.

If you want that Cadillac automobile, cut a photograph of the type and style car. Post it on the wall. Get yourself an Omni-Cosmic Bulletin Board. Hang it in your den or meditation area. Look at the picture of the car.

See yourself on a bright sunny day riding in it along the countryside. Feel happy and confident that you were able to obtain it. Make the car a truth in your own mind. Somehow you will be able to obtain it through your mental processes which will turn on your OCP power to action and find one for you.

Carl M. did just that. He followed my instructions for he truly wanted a Cadillac car. He saw an ad one day for an estate car just like the one he had posted on his Omni-Cosmic Bulletin Board. The car had been in an accident and was in need of repair. Carl was a fine mechanic who understood everything about cars. He was able to buy it for $900.00 and fix it like new. The car's value was $7,800.00.

You can have that car of your dreams if you follow the same procedure.

CREATE YOUR FUTURE WITH YOUR OMNI-COSMIC TELEGRAM

2. *I Create*—March-Ee-Ah, Spirit of the Dream World, bring my dream creations to a reality. I know you have the power to do so. My dreams are a blueprint of my future and I know you can act upon them to get my Higher Mind to respond to my mental thoughts. Thank you so much for your help. March-Ee-Ah. So let it be.

If you wish to travel to some exotic place, go to a travel agency and get some travel folders of the place. Put the pictures on your Omni-Cosmic Bulletin Board. Feel you have already arrived there. Create the trip in your mind.

Carolyn G. did just that. She had always wanted to travel and see exotic places. Carolyn did not have any money or even a job. I suggested that she try my

OCP ritual through her Omni-Cosmic Telegram method. I also suggested that she start looking for a job as well as posting some travel folders on her Omni-Cosmic Bulletin Board. She could thus create the trip and the job she wanted.

Carolyn followed my advice and within two weeks she found a job as a companion for a lady going to Bermuda. This woman traveled a great deal in this country and abroad. This was just the job for Carolyn for now she had a job, travel and a new life full of excitement and adventure. It was not luck, but the fact that she was able to create all this and believe it would happen.

Man saw birds fly in the sky and dreamed one day he would fly and because of this an airplane was created.

The creation is in your own mind. This is the stepping stone to your future.

Sit quietly and daydream about your life. See that perfect man or career complete in every detail and you will actually create it and draw it to be a reality.

Daydreams will bring you wealth and help you find all you want. Have a goal in mind. Center your whole attention on that goal. You will stir up the Omni-Cosmic psychic forces to bring it to you.

CHALLENGE YOURSELF WITH YOUR OMNI-COSMIC TELEGRAM

3. *I Challenge*—Mat-Ay-Sto-Zo, Spirit of New Adventure, help me find my desires ahead so that I may find all my wishes unfolding around me. I know nothing is impossible. I will accomplish all I want and seek. Send me new ideas that will help the world as well as myself. Thank you, May-Ay-Sto-Zo. So let it be.

The person who creates something in his mind, brings it into his experience, and then has the nerve to follow his dreams to help all those around him as well as himself in an unselfish way is a great individual. He will have the adventure and fun of it too.

Become a doing person who knows he can change the world for the better. See yourself accepting a challenge in a new career. See that man you want asking you out for a date and falling in love with you. Seek out that challenge in your life. It will happen if you just give it a little patience and time.

I did this and won. I saw myself lecturing all over the country as a well known psychic. I saw myself in front of large audiences very much in command of myself giving lectures that stirred people on.

Within a year my dreams materialized. It was a challenge and my deeper mind accepted it and followed through for me. I lectured in this country as well as in Canada and England.

I did it—so can you.

Natalie invoked her OCP power for a new home and received it through her winning ticket

Natalie C. had wanted a new home for a long time. She came to see me for a consultation. I felt she could have one if she would send out her OCP power command with an Omni-Cosmic Telegram for her dream home.

Our local home show had a brand new dream home as first prize. Natalie decided she wanted the home. She put a picture of it on her Omni-Cosmic Bulletin Board. Every day she saw herself living in this new home believing it had already happened.

She did this ritual for one month. Then the drawing for the home came. Lo and behold, Natalie was the winner. The new home was hers to live in. She had stirred her OCP power to action and now has the home of her dream creation. It was a challenge, but remember, nothing is impossible if you believe you can accomplish it.

PROJECT YOUR WILL WITH YOUR OMNI-COSMIC TELEGRAM FOR IMMEDIATE RESULTS

4. *I Will* rise to great heights ahead. Pee-See-Kat-Te, Spirit of Accomplishment and Recognition, help me complete my plans that I have willed in my life. I will be positive in all things. I know that you can help me reach my goals. I will achieve recognition and success in this world. I also want to help my fellow man through my successful accomplishments for I will not be selfish, but will give service to those around me. Thank you, Pee-See-Kat-Te, for your help. So mote it be.

Your OCP Telegram will send explosive action to your psychic electrons and cause things to happen. You are part of the Universal Plan that works in this matter.
You will have all you want. See it in your mind.
It will come to pass!

DECREE POSITIVE COMMANDS AND THEY WILL COME TO PASS

Say each Omni-Cosmic Telegram ten times each day for excellent results:

5. "*I Decree* — Pass-Pea-Ay, Spirit of Positive Forces, grant me the following decrees so I may find happiness in time ahead.

I decree wealth for myself.
I decree happiness for me and those around me.
I decree good health.

**I decree success all around me.
I decree prominence in my community for myself.
I decree greatness for myself in all I do.
I decree successful living for myself and those I love.
Thank you Pass-Pea-Ay. So mote it be.**

Feed these Omni-Cosmic Telegrams to your deeper mind. Digest and absorb them in a quiet meditative mood for a few minutes each day. You will see success and recognition coming in your direction in no time.

Visualize yourself as a wealthy person walking down the street in your city, seeing people turn around to look at you because you are a prominent person in the community.

See that expensive country club you always wanted to belong to accept you as one of the social set.

See your abilities and talents magnified and yourself successful and receiving recognition in your field of endeavor.

See your body slim, healthy and vibrant.

See your family and friends happy and loving you, for you are important to the community and your own family circle.

Know you will give something to the world. Love humanity and make your life worth living and find inner happiness.

I did it—so can you

I did this in my own community. I was unknown, but believed so much in my ability. I wanted to become a prominent person and did.

I visualized myself on TV and radio and appearing in local and national newspaper articles. All of this occurred within a six-month period.

When I am out shopping or in a restaurant or any public place, people stop and look for they know they have seen me before, either on TV or in a newspaper article. It happens all the time and I just love the attention. You can do it too.

Become that successful person you always wanted to be. Your mind is the most powerful instrument you have available.

USE YOUR OMNI-COSMIC TELEGRAM TO FIND YOUR GREATEST ACCOMPLISHMENTS

6. *I Find*—Tay-Noo-Toe, Spirit of New Discoveries, help me unfold new and creative ideas. I will develop all of my mind potential and find out all the secrets of this universe for making money come to me in abundance. I will find the Midas touch and have all the riches I desire and need. Thank you, Tay-Noo-Toe. So let it be.

Use the words *I Find* to help start the action within your deeper mind with your Omni-Cosmic Telegram. You will start the money flow. It will come to you in the form of new ideas and discoveries of all types that will lead you to your pile of riches.

Michael found a warmer climate, a new job and greater income

Michael J. was unhappy about the cold winters in Albany, N.Y. He wanted a hot dry climate. He posted photographs of Arizona on his Omni-Cosmic Bulletin Board. He would visualize a large ranch home with a kidney-shaped swimming pool that he could use year round.

Michael kept reassuring himself every day with his Omni-Cosmic Telegram on how much he loved the climate, his new income and his new home.

Michael did this for six weeks and one day his supervisor called him to see the president of the corporation he worked for, who offered him a position in Arizona for $10,000 more a year than he was making in Albany. He was to head a new plant out there. Of course he accepted it. He now has more money, prestige, a warm dry climate and a new life style which he loves.

BECOME A WINNER IN LIFE

Learn to use the Omni-Cosmic Telegrams to reach out and get what you want in life. It may be a fine home, beautiful clothes, an expensive car, or any other luxury you may desire.

Become a winner in life. Win that job you have always wanted. Win the love of that man you have secretly loved at a distance. Win the approval of your fellow man socially so you will be accepted to membership in the social club you always wanted to be part of. Win that trip you have dreamed of so long. It is easy once you try it through your Omni-Cosmic Psychometrics.

Lawyer reverses his bad luck

Tom J., a lawyer I went to college with, was not doing well with many of his court cases. It seemed nothing had gone his way in the last six months. He was constantly losing his court battles.

Tom called me one day and asked me for help. He said, "What am I doing wrong? I keep losing court cases. Lately, my opponent always overpowers me in court!"

Tom felt he had a curse. I told him, "No, I feel you have done a great deal of negative thinking in the last year and this is the result. Use my Omni-Cosmic Telegram and you will find your luck changing. You will start to win your legal battles again in court."

He said to me, "Ann, I will try anything. Tell me what to do." I gave him the following ritual to say each morning:

7. *I Win*—Lar-Get-Too, Spirit of Success and Honor, help me win all my legal cases ahead for the coming year.

I will do my best for each client. I will receive high settlement of money in each case. My income will be higher than it has ever been. I will be a help to my client and to my community. Thank you, Lar-Get-Too. So let it be.

Tom was a winner in the next year. He won every case. His income doubled within that time period. He made $200,000 by learning how to condition his subconscious mind to the right thinking patterns and this was the result.

You can be a winner in life by using your Omni-Cosmic Telegrams. There is no need to lack success or money. It is there for the taking if you know how to tap it.

POINTS TO REMEMBER

1. You can be powerful enough to turn your thoughts into riches, for your mental power can bring you all the money and wealth you want by tapping your Omni-Cosmic Psychometrics.
2. You will be able to achieve the Midas touch in your life.
3. I have found wealthy people all have the same mental attitude belief and desire. They know how to direct their minds by using certain mental thought commands which have led them to money, recognition, and success.
4. Your subconscious mind is aware of everything around you. The key is programming your mind with the right words that represent power and wealth. This starts the action.
5. Your subconscious mind links with the Universal Mind for all this is a part of the OCP power which is within each of us.
6. Use the seven Omni-Cosmic Telegrams that will start your OCP power functioning. Repeat the proper Omni-Cosmic Telegram out loud five times and then sit quietly and say it over five times mentally. Call the proper spirit force to stir up your mental machinery which will bring it to a reality.
7. The wealth of the universe is all around you. You just have to call it to action when you need it.
8. Feed the Omni-Cosmic Telegrams to your deeper mind. Digest and absorb them in a quiet meditative mood for a few

minutes each day. You will see success and recognition coming in your direction in no time.

9. You will have all you want. See it in your mind. Post it on your Omni-Cosmic Bulletin Board. It will come to pass.
10. Carl did this and was able to get the car of his dreams by using his Omni-Cosmic Telegram—*I Wish*.
11. Carolyn was able to find a job, travel and new life full of excitement and adventure by using her Omni-Cosmic Telegram—*I Create*. She found the creative was in her mind, which is the stepping stone to the future.
12. Natalie was able to win her dream home through the Omni-Cosmic Telegram—*I Challenge*. She stirred her OCP power to action. It was a challenge for her but remember nothing is impossible if you believe you can accomplish it.
13. You will rise to great heights by using the Omni-Cosmic Telegram *I Will*. You will have all you want. See it in your mind. It will come to pass.
14. Decree positive commands and they will come to pass. Use the Omni-Cosmic Telegram—*I Decree*. I did it—so can you.
15. Michael found a warmer climate, a new job and greater income by using Omni-Cosmic Telegram—*I Find*.
16. We can all become winners in life. Use the Omni-Cosmic Telegram—*I Win* and it will change your luck for positive results.
17. Tom, a young lawyer I know, was able to reverse his bad luck with court cases by using Omni-Cosmic Telegram—*I Win*. He not only won every case, but doubled his income by learning how to condition his subconscious mind with the right thinking patterns.
18. You can become the person you want to be by using Omni-Cosmic Telegrams. Start today for luck, happiness and wealth.

Chapter 13

Looking into the Future with Omni-Cosmic Psychic Power for Rewards Now!

Would you like to be able to look into the future?

Would you like to know in advance about the various opportunities, the money you can obtain, the new and interesting people you will meet, and the long and healthy life you will have?

It is possible to do this.

Now you are at a point where you will be able to look into your future and see what is ahead. In this way you will be able to direct yourself through problems that may present themselves and make decisions. You will know when you are lucky and take full advantage of this.

As you proceed in this chapter you will look ahead and shape your life into anything you desire.

IS IT POSSIBLE TO SEE INTO THE FUTURE?

This has been one of the profound questions all through the ages. Is it possible for a person to see the future? Yes, it is possible through Omni-Cosmic psychic power which we call clairvoyance or psychic seeing. Your Omni-Cosmic Psychic Power helps to activate the energy patterns in your mind so you will know all things ahead, as well as things past and also in the present.

Omni-Cosmic Psychic Power will give you the chance to move the time barrier, to go beyond time and space with the help of your spirit guides and your magic sage. You will be informed and in this way you will be able to improve your life.

We have several paths to the future. If you know what they are you will be sure to pick the right one. Imagine a road with many paths leading to a central point. It is the same way with a person's future. You can change your destiny if you are informed about it. A right decision can bring you a life of happiness. A wrong decision can bring you disaster.

YOUR MAGIC SAGE WILL SHOW YOU THE FUTURE

It is so easy if only you will tune into your future through your Magic Sage Ritual. Invite your Magic Sage to help you as you tune ahead with your own mind.

He knows the future so just call on his help. Ask your Magic Sage to sit across from you and show you the details on the mental screen you will draw in your mind. It will be just like seeing a movie or looking at a TV screen, viewing the action coming into your life.

After you say your Magic Sage Ritual, let your mind drift, draw a blank white screen in your mind. Let the energy flow to you with details and scenes of the future. If the future events are not on the subject you are concerned with, ask him to change the information coming through. Your Magic Sage has the power to do this.

Sit quietly in a relaxed position in a straight chair and let your mind give you the details you have requested. You will be surprised how clear your thoughts will become after you do this a few times. You will also be amazed with your own accuracy.

When your ritual time of 15 minutes is over, write all the details in your Omni-Cosmic Forecast Notebook (you can use a stenographer's notebook with a divided line in the middle), so you will be able to check your predictions at a later time. When you develop this technique after a little practice, you will be able to come out with a score of 85-90 percent in your accuracy. In some cases you may even score 100 percent!

Joyce was saved from suicide by looking into her future

Joyce R., a teacher I know from Springfield, Massachusetts, was so unhappy that she could not see anything ahead for herself. Her boyfriend had been killed in an accident two months before she came to see me at my office for a consultation. She felt no one would ever do for her again. Her purpose in life had ended.

That day she came to see me, she had dark circles under her eyes and she looked like a total wreck instead of the beautiful redhead I had known in the past.

I told her that she should ask her Magic Sage for help, for her spirit guide would be able to look into her future and show her what was ahead. In this way she would be able to tackle her problems and overcome her unhappiness. I said to her, "Your future is bright if you will only give it time and believe in what your Magic Sage will show you in your mind."

Joyce did the Magic Sage Ritual described in Chapter 3 and told me that he said to her, "Within four weeks you will meet a man who will be right for you and he will change your life and bring it meaning." He also showed her an outline of the man in her mind.

Within 28 days, to be exact, Joyce was invited to a party in another city nearby and decided to go. At the party she found a man who was just the type her Magic Sage had showed in her mind that day she had reached out for help.

It was a good thing she had tried to look somewhat like the beautiful girl she had been just a few months ago.

Not only did the man, whose name was David like her, but he dated her for the next three months steadily. Then he proposed to Joyce. He is a successful businessman who can do a lot for her and give her the security and love she needs. Of course they married, and I stood up for them. Joyce admitted to me later, "I was so foolish to think of suicide when all I had to do was to ask my Magic Sage to look ahead and show me the answers. Thank you, Ann, for giving me the insight to do this."

David and Joyce are very happy today. Now they have two lovely children, two dogs, a beautiful home and a very workable marriage.

How a widower found his future wife

Simon D., a widower I know, was obsessed with the idea of finding the right woman. He really wanted to remarry. He had dated several women in the three years since his wife died, but he could not find the right one. He felt his three children needed a mother and he needed a companion for himself. He knew the right woman would bring him the happiness he so badly wanted.

He was very upset the day he came to see me professionally. He felt that it was hopeless. He said to me, "I will never find another woman that I can love and will return love to me. Ann, I have been looking for the right one and it never seems to happen. I do not know what to do."

I answered, "Simon, it is so easy. All you have to do is call your Magic Sage and he will show you the woman and how to meet her. I feel you will meet this woman within the next six or seven weeks. Simon agreed and used the Magic Sage ritual for guidance in his problem.

Simon was told by his Magic Sage after five days of using the ritual that he would find the right woman within the next two months. He instructed him to join a tennis club. It would be there he would meet this woman. Within the time period of six weeks to be exact, he saw a lady who fit the description of the one he had seen on his mind screen. He knew this was the right one.

He met Karen and dated her for six months. After that time, he asked her to be his wife for he felt so happy when he was with her. They married and it has been a very successful relationship. Simon found his Magic Sage responded and showed him a glimpse of the future. He went ahead and carried it out. Your Omni-Cosmic psychic power will never fail if you have faith in it.

How Ralph solved his job decision

Ralph K., a young sales executive, had been looking around for a better job for over six months. Suddenly he had three job offers all at once. He had a matter of two days to make a decision. Each one seemed to have its own merits. Ralph was in a confused state for he did not want to make a mistake and select the wrong one.

Ralph had been one of my students in a past class. He had learned all about calling his Magic

Sage for help and guidance. Because he needed a prompt answer and he could not get in touch with me (I was out of town at a conference) Ralph called upon the Magic Sage immediately. He remembered what I had taught in class, that your Magic Sage is always there to help you.

The first night Ralph's Magic Sage showed him the outcome of one of the jobs. He would become an important member of the firm and would be in line for a vice presidency in five years. Ralph chose that job which, in turn, did work out just the way he had been shown. Remember, your Magic Sage always knows the best route to success in life. Call upon him and he will come quickly. He can see the future clearly.

HOW TO DETERMINE TIME IN A FUTURE SITUATION

First you must get an impression of an event occurring in your life. When you get this information about the event that you may have seen or felt ahead, you then ask your Magic Sage to be more definite. Hold a conversation with him so you can get the date. This will help you in working out your future.

If you cannot get the information about the date in this way, place a calendar in front of you and look ahead in time to see if January, February, March, etc. give you a feeling as you tune in ahead. Ask him to impress you with the right month. For example if you feel March is the month, then go by day 1, 2, 3, 4, 5, 6, etc. until you get a feeling. After you get the date worked around in your mind, ask yourself if the right answer is early or late in the month and what week of the month to check yourself.

In this way you can actually get time to the very day so you will be prepared for it when it occurs. It is better to be prepared and not surprised with many situations in life, for you will be able to handle them more effectively.

If you really get persistent, you can get it to the time of day. I do not feel this is necessary for it takes too much time, but if you try it, you can do it. I have only done this when a special need for preciseness was necessary.

Remember to record all your data in your Omni-Cosmic Forecast Notebook to prove out your feelings so you will build your confidence. Time and patience will pay off when you learn to tune in your Omni-Cosmic Psychic power.

I found my husband through my Omni-Psychic Power

You may be surprised to learn that I had not been lucky in love in my early 20's. I used my Magic Sage Ritual after researching some old Tibetan records eight years ago to show me the man I would marry and where to find him.

My Magic Sage showed a summer resort in the Airondacks that I should go to on a vacation. He showed me a man with light hair who would become interested in me and later marry me.

I followed through with my vision of the future and three weeks later at that particular resort I met my husband, Richard, just the way it had unfolded in my mind.

We married three months later and always talk about how we happened to go to that particular resort where most of the couples were 60 or over and married. Our chances for meeting a single young person were very slim, but I know my Magic Sage directed both of us to go to the same place to meet. I feel my Magic Sage created the situation for me to find a husband and it worked.

Clifford desperately needed money, so he looked into his future and found the amount he needed

Clifford needed money for insurance and taxes. He was in a very depressed, unhappy state of mind. He was on the verge of bankruptcy at this point, too. I suggested he use his Magic Sage Ritual to show him the way to get the money he needed.

His Magic Sage showed him a racing form and the day he should go to the races and win. He followed his vision and did just what he had been shown. That day at the races he made $1,200.00 which covered the taxes and insurance due.

He uses this method whenever he needs extra money. His Magic Sage always responds and helps him. It has made his life more satisfying.

IN TIME YOU WILL NOT NEED YOUR MAGIC SAGE TO SEE THE FUTURE

Your Magic Sage will come as long as he is needed. As your Omni-Cosmic Psychic Power grows and unfolds you will not always need to call him. You will gain confidence in your predictions and thus do it all yourself.

Any time you need help your Magic Sage will always respond. You will become less dependent as time goes on.

As your future unfolds you will control all the forces around you. This universe is yours to do with what you wish as you learn to open and direct your Omni-Cosmic Psychic Power channels.

Sam was healed of a serious condition by seeing the future

A friend of mine, Sam W., believes that his Magic Sage saved his life and I feel he did, too. About a year and half ago Sam had a chest condition that did not seem to clear up. He thought it was just a bad chest cold. After a month it seemed the condition was worse not better.

Sam had been a student of mine and decided to call upon his Magic Sage to see what kind of an answer he would get about his health problem.

His Magic Sage answered him the same day and said to Sam, "You have a case of pneumonia. Go to the emergency room of your nearest hospital tonight before your condition gets any worse. You need an antibiotic immediately." Sam became alarmed and did just what he was told.

Sam had planned to go to his doctor the following week if his chest did not clear up. The doctor at the hospital told him he was lucky he came in when he did. Next week would have been too late. Sam recovered quickly. In a week he was much better.

Sam felt that his Magic Sage had saved his life by helping him see the future and getting him to go for medical help when he did. Do you feel Sam changed his future? I feel he did because he could have waited too long and found himself on the other side. Sometimes the future can be changed when you can see what is ahead. His Magic Sage had future knowledge and helped Sam to recover and have a happy, healthy life.

Katy looks into the future to check on trips

Katy M., a personal friend of mine, always calls upon her Magic Sage to see ahead for her when she wants to go on a trip, whether by plane, train or car.

Some may say it is silly but she always feels assured and safe after she does this. One time her Magic Sage looked ahead and advised her not to take a bus trip to New York City the next day. Katy canceled her plans. The bus had an accident. Five people were killed and ten went to the hospital. Katy saved herself from a tragedy.

Katy will say this ritual to her Magic Sage when she calls him.

I ask my Magic Sage to help me on a decision to travel. Will I have a favorable trip (date)? Will I return in good health? Will I be happy that I took this trip? Thank you for your help.

Katy will get an answer right away for she has done this many times. She always goes by his reply. She has found the information received in the past to be accurate.

Try this method before you go on your next trip. You will be able to avoid trouble, accidents or bad health.

You will be able to know the future so you can get the most out of your life.

POINTS TO REMEMBER

1. You will be able to look ahead into your future and see what lies in your life's path. In this way you will be able to direct yourself through problems and make decisions that may present themselves.
2. It is possible through Omni-Cosmic Psychic Power to see psychically. Your Omni-Cosmic Psychic Power helps to activate the energy patterns in your mind so you will know all things ahead, as well as things past and also in the present.
3. Omni-Cosmic Psychic Power will give you the chance to move the time barrier, to go beyond time and space with the help of your spirit guides and your Magic Sage. You will be informed, and in this way you will be able to improve your life.
4. We have several paths to the future. If you know what they are, you will be sure to pick the right one. Imagine a road with many paths leading to a central point.

5. It is the same with a person's future. You can change your destiny if you are informed about it. A right decision can bring you a life of happiness. A wrong decision can bring you disaster.
6. Use your Magic Sage Ritual to tune into your future and you will be shown what lies ahead on your mental screen.
7. After you have said your Magic Sage Ritual let your mind drift, draw a blank white screen in your mind and let the energy flow to see what information will be given to you.
8. Write down all the details received in your Omni-Cosmic Forecast Notebook so you can check your predictions at a later time. With a little practice you will score an accuracy of 85 to 90 percent in most cases.
9. You will get a definite time if you hold a conversation with your Magic Sage or use a calendar to let him influence your mind for the right answers.
10. Joyce was saved from suicide by calling on her Magic Sage so she could look into her future.
11. Simon found his future wife when his Magic Sage responded and showed him a glimpse of his future. Today he is a happily married man.
12. Ralph had three job offers. He was able to chose the right one with the help of his Magic Sage.
13. I found my husband through my Omni-Cosmic Psychic Power. I followed through on my vision of the future and three weeks later we met at a particular resort I had seen on my mind screen. We married three months later. My Magic Sage created the situation for me to find a husband.
14. Clifford desperately needed money so he looked into his future and found the amount he needed.
15. In time you will not need your Magic Sage, for as your Omni-Cosmic Psychic Power unfolds and grows, you will gain the confidence in your own predictions and do it all yourself.
16. Sam was healed of a serious health condition by seeing into his future.
17. Start today to check out your future with your Magic Sage and you will reap great rewards in life.

Chapter 14

Using Omni-Cosmics to Travel Astrally to Discover Miraculous Secret Knowledge and Break the Time Barrier

Omni-Cosmics will enable you to travel astrally to distant places, to tune in on conversations at great distances and to see what is happening in other parts of the world. It will cost you nothing and you can do and see so much.

You will be able to learn the secrets of your past lives or tap the mysteries of the universe. You may have some psychic visions that you will remember when you awaken. These visions may help you find out what dangers lie ahead so they can be avoided.

During your astral travel you will be able to go beyond the dimensions of time and space. You may contact people who are living as well as those in the spirit world.

You will find all kinds of secret information which you can use for your benefit. It is there within your reach!

WHAT HAPPENS WHEN YOU TRAVEL ASTRALLY

When you travel astrally you will hear, feel and see things around you with your Spirit Body while your Physical Body is relaxed and at ease in your own bed.

Your body will function properly while you travel astrally in a floating manner. You will feel weightless and can go from one place to another in a matter of seconds. Your physical body will be at home and at rest. You will go through doors and walls and be transparent if you desire or be seen when you want to be. You will remember everything that happened while you were out of your body on the astral flight.

Traveling astrally is fun and safe. There is no danger in this if you protect yourself before you leave on your astral flight. You will not get trapped nor will you fail to return to your physical body when you have completed your journey.

HOW TO TRAVEL ASTRALLY USING OMNI-COSMICS

Your Omni-Cosmic Psychic Power will get into an astral flight very easily and simply. Here is what to do:

First of all use your Omni-Cosmic Protecto-Ray as described in Chapter 6, employing your Omni-Cosmic Psychic Radar Beams to turn it on. This is the most important step for your bodily protection. Negative forces will not be able to invade your physical body when you travel in your spirit body.

Next lie on a bed and let your conscious mind become completely passive. Fix your attention on where you wish to go on your astral flight. For practice, select a chair in your room which is at least six feet away from the bed and will yourself to sit in it.

Next day follow this ritual before you attempt to leave on your astral trip:

I ask Mor-so, the Spirit that directs and controls the astral world, to allow me entrance there so I may be

free to travel and have access to all that is available. I wish to explore the dimension of the future through time and space and also explore mysteries of my past lives. I wish to be given valuable information on whatever I have on my mind and cannot solve without your help. My power words are "Nam-Yo-Fara-On." Thank you, Mor-so. So let it be.

Close your eyes and become relaxed. To be successful you will have to rid yourself of fear. There will be some vibrational sounds, followed by a blank period and then you will be aware of being outside of your body.

You will be able to see your physical body lying on the bed while you will be floating in the air. Do not struggle or fight for you will be able to move freely and quickly in your astral body.

It is best to experiment at night when your activities are over for the day and you can fully relax. Practice this every day for about 15 minutes and after a short time you will be able to do this at will.

Write down all your experiments so you can recall them for further evaluation. As you do this you will find facts to better and enrich your life and create new situations in your world.

You will be able to get your higher mind to solve problems. You may ask it for guidance in your personal life or in your business, or you may become creative in art, writing or music.

Thomas Edison is known to have worked out some of his most difficult problems when he went on an astral trip. When he awoke he would write down all the details he had received and thus he was able to give the world so much.

IT IS SO EASY TO TRAVEL ASTRALLY AND SEE PLACES YOU HAVE NEVER BEEN TO

You will get away from your humdrum life and go anywhere you want in a matter of seconds. It is your thought that will bring you to your destination and also bring you back equally as fast to your physical body. You think yourself from place to place and you can also visit your loved ones in the spirit world.

When you take your astral flights use them to get as much information as possible. See foreign lands and famous buildings as the Taj Mahal in India, the Parthenon in Greece, or the Coliseum in Italy.

You may write down what you wish to see or just let yourself drift into the place where you want to be. Your astral body will be able to carry you there in a very short time.

Sometimes you will arrive at a different place that you did not plan to visit. You may feel it was just a dream, but you will be able to remember all the scenes vividly. It is an exciting way to travel. Try it.

When you return to your physical body, it is the end of your astral flight. Your mind directs the action. It is like a plane landing; suddenly you will awaken and it will all seem like a dream.

How Judith passed the professional career test by taking an astral flight

Judith K. needed to pass the professional career test to hold her job with the State Department. She desperately needed the job for her husband was crippled and his disability checks were not enough to meet bare living expenses.

Many times in the past she had known what it was to be without food for a day. Her home was clean, but lacked the luxuries most people have, such as a TV set, or a washing machine. She had not purchased a new outfit in the last two years because of her tight money situation.

Judith studied earnestly for the exam. If she did not pass, she would be replaced by another person in the department who had her eye on her job.

Judith came in to see me for a consultation and I suggested she try her Omni-Cosmic Astral Travel Ritual to help her pass the test. She followed my instructions and one night, after a week of using the ritual, she saw the man holding the exam in his hands for approval. The test was within three days.

She was able to see all the questions on the exam and when she awoke she wrote them down so they would be fixed in her mind when she took the exam. Of course she passed with a very high score, kept her job and has since gone on to a higher position. Her income has increased too.

Judith now has some of the luxuries she could not afford two years ago. The Omni-Cosmic Astral Travel Ritual really paid off for her.

Jim recovered $20,000 through an Omni-Cosmic astral flight

Jim was not a very rich man, but he had loaned some of his life savings to a friend, Bill, who had promised to return it with 10 percent interest in 90 days.

Bill never came through with the money. He cried poverty and told Jim he had lost all the money in bad investments.

Jim did not buy the story for he knew Bill was still living in an elegant apartment, driving an expensive car and going out to dine in exclusive restaurants every week.

Jim consulted me and decided to take an Omni-Cosmic Astral Flight to Bill's apartment to check on his worth and to see if he had any bank books. Jim did have a signed receipt for the debt.

Jim's lawyer had checked with local banks and could not find any money on deposit. Jim found two

New York City bank books with $90,000 on deposit. He went back to his lawyer and gave the name of the banks and the account numbers and asked him to check it out.

Bill was called into court for fraud and failure to pay off the note he had signed. Jim won the case and was paid his $20,000 with all the interest due.

If Jim had not been aware of his Omni-Cosmic Astral Travel Ritual he would not have been able to recover the money.

Herman found $500,000 his father had hidden on their ranch in Arizona

Herman, one of my students, started to use his Omni-Cosmic Astral Travel Ritual and practiced so much he was able to travel and use this ability quickly, any time he wanted. Practice makes perfect when you do this.

Herman's father had died in Arizona and had left very little money in his estate. Herman knew his father was wealthy, but miserly, and did not trust banks. He felt he had hidden the money on the ranch. The ranch was up for sale to settle the estate. Herman knew he had to find it soon or someone else would own the land.

He decided to go there by astral travel and look around to see if he could spot the money. He went through the roof from room to room looking for a hiding place for the money. He saw a large armoire in his father's bedroom and his psychic sense told him to look there. He saw a stack of bills in a false bottom of the armoire amounting to one-half million in $100 and $50 bills. He received the amount of the money psychically.

Herman took a plane to the ranch so he could go in his physical body and claim the money. The armoire he had seen in his father's room was not to be seen in the room. After he investigated a little further he found a hidden partition in the bedroom (In your astral body you can go through walls without any effort.) He followed what he had seen on the astral flight and found the money. He was overjoyed and split the money with his sister and two brothers. This helped to cut the inheritance tax on the money he had found.

His astral flight paid off, and for a young man of 25 he made some very sound investments in the stock market which paid off royally. His future is secure and his father is happy on the other side because his children now have use of the money he left behind.

I found my grandfather's will for my family

Five years ago my grandfather on my mother's side died. The family could not find a will. My grandfather had been a very secretive person. Many of the relatives were trying to cut in on his estate because of no will being found. Psychically I could feel there was a will in a hidden safe deposit box.

I decided to use my Astral Flight Ritual to contact him on the other side. I willed myself to go to the spirit world and found my grandfather waiting for me.

I talked to him just as if he were here with me in person on this plane of life. He told me, "Ann, I did leave a will. I hid it in a safe deposit box in New York City. You will find the key taped under the top drawer of the nightstand in my bedroom. Go find the key and get the will. I want my money to be

Using Omni-Cosmics to Travel Astrally 171

divided as stated in the will. I was wrong in being so mistrusting and not leaving it where you and the family could have found it easily. Thank you so much for coming here to see and talk with me, Ann. Now I will be happy."

I went to my grandfather's house to look for the key. It was there just as he said it would be. I gave it to my mother who turned it over to the lawyer who was handling the estate. The will was found just where he told me it would be. I was able to go beyond time and space to the fourth dimension to talk to my dead grandfather. By the way, I was mentioned in the will and received a small inheritance.

Melvin sees his future restaurant

When you take an astral flight at night, you will be able to get a clairvoyant vision of your future life. You will see the present and know how your future will unfold. It will help you go in the right direction.

Melvin, 39 and a friend of mine, used this technique to see ahead in his life. He had a strong desire to become wealthy. He had worked many long years as a waiter in a well-known restaurant in my city. He was married with two children. During this time he had managed to save $12,000 by being thrifty because he knew he needed a nest egg to make his fortune.

Melvin wanted to see his future to see how he would use his savings to become financially wealthy. One night he took an astral flight that showed him his future. He saw beaches, palm trees, oranges and many elegant hotels. He knew he was in Southern California. Then he saw the name of a restaurant spelled out in his mind. He knew this was the place he would buy and make his fortune. He went to Palm Springs that year for a vacation.

He found that there was a restaurant with the name he had seen in his mind. It had been closed since the owner's death and was for sale. Melvin was able to borrow some money from his relatives and with the money he had saved he went into the restaurant business. His restaurant became well known and its fame spread for its excellent cuisine and ambiance. Within three years, Melvin had enough money to buy another restaurant. The following year he opened two more restaurants. Today he is worth well over one million dollars. Melvin was able to go ahead in time to see what he could do to make his fortune and he did it.

POINTS TO REMEMBER

1. You can use Omni-Cosmics to travel astrally to distant places to tune in on conversations at great distances and to see what is happening in other parts of the world. Best of all, it costs you nothing.
2. You will be able to learn the secrets of your past lives or tap the mysteries of the universe. You may have some psychic visions that you will remember when you awaken.
3. You will be able to travel beyond time and space during your astral trip. You can contact people in the living as well as in the spirit world.
4. Omni-Cosmic Astral travel will enable you to find all kinds of information which you can use for your own benefit.
5. When you travel astrally you will hear, see and feel things around you in your astral body while your physical body is relaxed and at ease in your bed.
6. You will feel weightless and can go from one place to another in a matter of seconds. You will go through walls and doors and be transparent and have complete recollection of what has happened while you were out of your body.

7. Astral travel is fun and safe. There isn't any danger in it if you protect yourself before you leave on your astral flight by using your Omni-Cosmic Protecto-Ray. Your Omni-Cosmic Psychic Radar Beams will turn it on.
8. Lie on a bed and let your mind become passive. Say your Omni-Cosmic Astral Flight Ritual and direct your mind where you want to go. With a little practice you will be able to do it any time you want to.
9. You will get away from your humdrum life and go anywhere you want to in a matter of seconds. You think yourself from place to place.
10. When you take your astral flights try to get as much information as possible. You will be able to visit foreign lands and see famous places abroad. Write down what you wish to see or just let yourself drift into the place you want to be. Your astral body will be able to carry you there in a very short time.
11. When you return to your physical body it is the end of your astral journey. Your mind directs the action. It is like a plane landing; suddenly you will awaken and it will all seem like a dream.
12. You will be able to find out facts to better and enrich your life and create new situations in your world.

Start today to enjoy your astral trips. They are free and available for the asking.

Chapter 15

Using Omni-Cosmic Psycho-Imagonics to See Through the Magic Mirror for Love, Power, Money, Health and Happiness

You are now advanced enough to project mental images on your magic mirror which will produce all the riches, love, power, health and happiness you wish to create in your life. It can be accomplished quickly and it is so easy to do.

With Omni-Cosmic Psycho-Imagonics (OCPI) you will be able to project a mental image of an idea or thought and create it by imagination alone. This is projected on your magic mirror to produce the results you seek. You wish by thinking and it is created for you. All you need is a little patience and belief. You will find the results unbelievable.

What negative imagination will do

Sam J., a butcher I know, one day was hanging a side of beef in his meat market. It slipped and the hook pierced his arm. Sam was in great agony and would not allow anyone to touch the arm. When his doctor examined the arm, he found it was not injured for the hook had only pierced the coat sleeve. This is what the power of imagination can do.

I know of a case where two men present at the exhumation of a body of a man who had been seriously ill for a long time became ill themselves at the time the coffin was being opened. They could feel and sense the odor of the decomposition of the body. Yet when the coffin was examined it was empty except for a small quantity of dirt and stone.

I know of two other men who were bitten by dogs. When they were told the dogs were mad they died from fear. Yet when the dogs were checked they did not have any trace of rabies.

Your thinking has great power. It has the power of life and death over you. It has to be directed along positive paths to produce the results that are good in life.

Thoughts can control you. Now is the time to learn to control them. This is what I will attempt to do for you in this chapter. Remember, I can direct you, but you must follow through yourself with your thinking.

HOW TO USE YOUR OMNI-COSMIC PSYCHO-IMAGONICS WITH YOUR MAGIC MIRROR

Hidden in your deeper mind is the power to achieve all your dreams. You have the power to accomplish this with OCPI.

The spirit you call upon will project the results on your magic mirror after you have said the ritual and developed the mental techniques that are acquired by meditation.

To construct your magic mirror get a good size piece of glass approximately 8" x 10". Paint the back of the glass with black spray paint. Let it dry overnight before you use it. Place it on a stand so you can have it in front of you when you are sitting in your chair. Gaze at it in a relaxed state of mind. Place two white candles, one on each side of your magic mirror. Have them lit when you do this for the white candles help direct the positive forces to you. They also help the spirit you call on in this ritual to accomplish what you have asked him to do for you.

USE THE FOLLOWING RITUAL

1. Sit in a comfortable chair. Try to achieve a relaxed state of mind. Simply tell yourself to relax all parts of your body from your head to your toes.

2. Take five deep breaths and as you do so you will find yourself getting more relaxed and slipping downward into a meditative state, forgetting everything around you. You are at this point turning yourself inward.

3. Draw a blank mental screen in your mind. Project what you wish to accomplish on your mental screen.

4. Then say the following ritual:

Nam Yo Fara On—Mo-ren-doe, Spirit of the world of Imagination and Magic hear and accept my request. I have my magic mirror before me. Show me what will come to me or what path I have to go to get my desire. I know you have the power to do this. I will achieve all that I seek. I know you will grant my request. Thank you, Mo-ren-doe. So let it be.

5. Sit for ten minutes and meditate. Look into your magic mirror for the answer. It will take a little time at first, but after a while you will be able to get all of your answers with this psychic technique. The spirit is there and available at your call. This is the method used by occultists for the evocative art of second sight.

Phyllis found her husband through Omni-Cosmic Psycho-Imagonics

Phyllis was a woman of 32 who was sad because her personal life was uneventful. She had not had a date in two years. She asked me, "Where can I find a suitable man?", the day she came to see me for advice about her future. I felt that she would meet someone soon.

I told her to use the Omni-Cosmic Psycho-Imagonics power ritual for more exciting details. I felt it would show her the future. Phyllis agreed to do this.

Phyllis used the ritual for one week. Then one night she saw in her magic mirror the name of a restaurant and a scene of a man sitting alone who would be in her future. He was well dressed, educated, good looking and lonely also.

Her magic mirror showed her that he would accidently brush against her while she was seated at a table as he was entering the restaurant.

Phyllis started to go to this restaurant alone each evening to see if such a man did go there for dinner. After four days she saw the man she had seen in her magic mirror entering the restaurant and he did just what she had seen—he brushed her arm as he walked by her table. He apologized and they started to talk to each other. He asked if he could join her for dinner.

He was an accountant and a graduate of Harvard University. He was just the type of man Phyllis had been looking for. They became friends and found they had many similar interests. Within five months he proposed to her. They married shortly thereafter. Today they are both very happy and it has been a meaningful marriage.

What happened was that Phyllis's spirit guide directed her to the right place to meet her future mate. She was able to see all the details through her magic mirror. She saw a glimpse of her future. It did materialize just as she had seen it.

Carlos needed money for his business debts and found it through his magic mirror

Carlos M., a young business man of 36, needed money to pay off some of his business debts or he would go under. Carlos had worked ten years to bring up the business to where it was, but due to a slow economy he was in debt over his head. He needed $15,000 within a month's time or he stood to lose all he had worked for in the last few years.

He needed help soon and an answer for what to do. He came to see me in a very depressed state of mind. He wanted to save his business if at all possible. I told him to say the Omni-Cosmic Psycho-Imagonic ritual and to make a magic mirror to see what his spirit guides would show him.

I felt it would be through a winning number that he would receive the money he needed. I also felt he would get the money within the month and save his business.

Carlos did the ritual for seven days and one day he saw on his magic mirror a horse race for the following day. He saw the number 9 which he felt stood for the ninth race. Then he saw three numbers in a row, 2 - 8 - 3. He felt this was the answer he had been waiting for. He placed a bet on the race and won $22,590.

Carlos had the money to pay his debts and to pay off his taxes to Uncle Sam and still had some money for a pleasure trip he badly needed. Everything came out fine for Carlos. He saved his business, of course, and has adopted a new outlook on life.

Today his business is doing very well. He is a happy, successful young man with a good future. He found a lovely wife and has just purchased a new home.

You can reverse the future when you adopt a positive attitude and really believe you can. There is help if you seek it out as Carlos did.

A real estate man doubled his sales with his Omni-Cosmic Psycho-Imagonics

Jerry K., a friend of mine, had devoted his career to selling real estate. He came to see me one day when his sales were down, very low. He did not know whether to stay in this field or go into another career. I felt he was good in his field. I also felt, as soon as I had tuned into his vibration, that he would be able to double his sales by using my OCPI ritual.

I felt he would be able to see his prospective customers in his magic mirror and see the ones who were really interested in buying a house or a business. By concentrating his efforts on the likely customers he would double his sales that year.

Jerry said he would give it a try for he really liked his work. Jerry would meditate and look into his magic mirror for the interested customers. He would give them the best sales talk and sell nine out of every ten of his leads. OCPI really paid off well for him.

Not only did his sales double, but also his income. He made $100,000 in the first six months after using my OCPI ritual.

You can do the same if you only try, and have a little patience.

YOUR MAGIC MIRROR OPENS UP NEW PATHWAYS

Look into your magic mirror for it will reflect the future. It will show you what is ahead. It is up to you to take advantage of it.

Your mind reflects the answers in the mirror of your soul. Then the images appear that will show you the way.

Omni-Cosmic Psycho-Imagonics is the key to cosmic wisdom which knows all, sees all and has all the universal knowledge. This will guide you. It will also show your destiny pattern.

Julie finds her diamond ring through Omni-Cosmic Psycho-Imagonics

Julie M., a client of mine, had mislaid a very expensive diamond ring which she had inherited from her mother's estate last year. She had looked all over her house but could not find it.

Julie sought my advice on this matter. I felt the ring was still in the house with some other papers in a container of some kind. She tried the OCPI ritual at my suggestion. I felt she would see the place where the ring was hidden and find it immediately. The very next day her magic mirror showed her the ring in a wastepaper basket near her dressing table. Luckily she had not emptied it out for a few days.

Julie found the ring among some papers in a container just as I had felt and she had seen on her magic mirror. She was overjoyed for it did have a sentimental value for her. This is just another way your OCPI ritual will help you in your everyday life.

I also felt that Julie's mother's spirit presence kept Julie from emptying the basket with the ring. Many times a spirit will protect a loved one because an article she owned in the past helps draw her to the area. This was the case with Julie.

Bernard became more energetic and overcame insomnia

Bernard M., a man I had met at a few parties some time ago, came to see me about his insomnia and lack of energy. He had dark circles around his eyes, generally did not look very healthy, and seemed years older than his actual age. He was upset about his children. He had a hectic life as an executive of a large corporation. He traveled a great deal and his responsibilities were heavy and demanding.

I suggested he try the OCPI ritual for relaxation and direction and to visualize better health. He did this for two months. He found his energy level increased. The dark circles disappeared, he was able to get more sleep at night, and he also had a calmer nature.

He was able to help his children with some of their problems and in general things worked out better in just this short period of time. When I met him two months later he looked ten years younger. I would say OCPI worked for him, for he had more insight and direction in life, and it also improved his basic health by calming his nerves.

You can do this also by imagining perfect health as you perform the OCPI ritual. It works if you set your thinking along positive lines and believe you can have good health.

Terry finds the man of her dreams through her magic mirror

Terry K., a young woman of 30, had been married and divorced three times. She needed love and companionship, but kept making mistakes by choosing the wrong man.

She came to see me for help in finding some direction in her life ahead. She had been unhappy and resentful to all of her husbands; thus each one was worse than the previous husband due to her negative thinking.

I told her to reverse her thinking and start forgiving each one of the men right away. This would clear up any negative thoughts she was holding within her mind. I told her to wish them all well so she could start her life anew.

The next step was to look into her magic mirror for the right husband so she could have the type of life she had so wanted and had been unable to find at this point.

Terry was operating on the law of attraction. Like attracts like. She had to give up her negativeness in order to attract a man who was positive to herself. She followed my instructions and within two months she took a cruise, and while she was on it, she met a doctor who had many similar interests. It was love at first sight.

They married within six months. It was truly a spiritual union of two people. This marriage lasted for Terry.

What had happened? Terry activated her psychic electrons which, in turn, carried the command to the universal mind which found the right man for her. Her magic mirror showed her the way.

You can do the same. The right man is out there for you too.

POINTS TO REMEMBER

1. With Omni-Cosmic Psycho-Imagonics you will be able to project a mental image of an idea or thought and create it by imagination alone. This is projected on your magic mirror to produce the results you seek.
2. You wish by thinking and it is created for you. All you need is a little patience and belief. You will find the results unbelievable.
3. Your thinking has great power. It has the power of life and death over you. It has to be directed along positive paths to produce the results that are good in life.
4. Thoughts can control you. Now is the time to learn to control them.
5. Hidden in your deeper mind is the power to achieve all your dreams. You have the power to accomplish this with OCPI power.
6. The spirit you call upon will project the results to you on your magic mirror after you have said the ritual and developed the mental techniques that are acquired by meditation.
7. Look into your magic mirror for it will reflect the future. It will show you what is ahead. It is up to you to take advantage of it.
8. Your mind reflects the answers in the mirror of your soul. Then the images will show you the way.
9. Omni-Cosmic Psycho-Imagonics is the key to cosmic wisdom which knows all, sees all and has all the universal knowledge.
10. It will guide you and show your destiny pattern.

Chapter 16

Tapping the Omni-Cosmic Power Channel to Release Miraculous Protective Psychic Powers

Tap your Omni-Cosmic Power Channel to achieve miraculous protective psychic power. It is available; just there to be used at your command.

Each day you will be able to turn on your Omni-Cosmic Power Channel to sense conditions around you. It is also necessary to surround your physical body with your Omni-Cosmic Protecto-Ray to protect your aura. This has been explained in Chapter 6.

HOW TO RELEASE YOUR PROTECTIVE PSYCHIC POWERS

First possess a strong belief that the Omni-Cosmic forces will protect you. You will find they do when you try them. I know it works for I have letters on file as well as testimonials from clients who have tried these protective methods. They find the power is there just for the asking.

You will be able to repel any negative forces that come into your vibration. Your mental state means a lot in this. It can make or break your opportunities in life as well as your safety.

Pick the right company for like attracts like—what you sow, so shall you reap. Start today to program a protective force around you using your Omni-Cosmic Power Channel and you will not have to fear anything at all.

Every day turn on your Omni-Cosmic Power Channel to keep your protective barriers up and keep you tuned into your environment. If you feel the need for more protection, use it four times daily to keep the protective psychic forces around you.

Say the following ritual:

Mi-Can-Toe—Spirit of the protective Omni-Cosmic forces of nature, hear my request for protection for this day. As I tune into my environment with my Omni-Cosmic Power Channel I will sense which direction to go for safety and productive accomplishment. I know you will stand by me and protect my body and use all the available Omni-Cosmic forces in the universe, for you have the power to do so. Thank you, Mi-Can-Toe. So let it be.

Now you are set for the day. You can expect the best things around you to appear without the interference of negative forces.

John was saved from drowning by using his Omni-Cosmic Power Channel

John K., a very good friend of mine who is a fair swimmer, went out too far one day in a lake. He became very tired and started to sink when he was out in the middle of the lake with no one in sight to help him. He was in the habit of using his Omni-

Cosmic Power Channel every day before he did anything else. He is a firm believer in tapping the Omni-Cosmic forces in nature.

Suddenly he felt a hand reach out to help him and he was brought back to shore. It worked for the Omni-Cosmic Power Channel sent out a signal for help and a spirit force came and pulled him out of the water to land. John did not know how he got back to shore for he had felt an invisible force carrying him over the top of the water to land safely.

HELP COMES FROM THE FOURTH DIMENSION

When you send out a call for help or assistance you will get aid from the spirit forces in the fourth dimension. Turn on your Omni-Cosmic Power Channel for help. It works quickly and effectively.

Send your protection signals and just let the universal forces come to your rescue.

I asked for help one day on a very important decision and within ten minutes the message came through so clearly I saved a lot of money and my career went in the right direction. You will find spirits in the next dimension—guardian angels ready and willing to help you day and night.

Wayne S., needed help one night when a robber was in his house. Wayne did not make any noise but silently turned on his Omni-Cosmic Power Channel in his head. He sent out some very powerful vibrations to get some help immediately.

A next-door neighbor decided to come over to see Wayne at the same time he was sending out the call for help. When the neighbor neared the house the thief fled without taking any of Wayne's belongings. When Wayne asked his friend, "How did you happen to come over when you did?" The neighbor replied, "All of a sudden I knew you needed me. Something in my mind said to me. 'Wayne needs you. Go over.' " The neighbor rushed over and was able to save Wayne from harm and loss of property.

Josephine needed help immediately with her husband when he was about to quit a job for one that was not stable. She used her Omni-Cosmic Power Channel for help from the next world. Her husband changed his mind about leaving the job within three days. This decision helped stabilize the marriage and his career. Josephine knows the Omni-Cosmic forces of the universe work fast for one's protection.

I was saved from being mugged through my Omni-Cosmic Power Channel

I always use my Omni-Cosmic Power Channel each day for the right direction and protection that I may need. If vibrations are heavy for that day I use it several times to insure adequate protection.

Two years ago I was invited to a Spiritual Frontiers Fellowship Christmas party in New York City at the Cathedral of St. John the Divine. When I stepped off the bus I realized the area was not desirable.

I immediately flashed on my Omni-Cosmic Power Channel as I was walking up the church steps. I found the door locked, but music could be heard within the building.

I went around to the side of the church which led to an alley. This door was locked also. Suddenly I turned around and two young boys, about 12 to 13 years of age, were right behind me. I smiled and said to them, "Sorry the doors are locked. It seems we cannot get into the church tonight." The two boys looked at me in a frightened way and took five steps backwards. Then they started to run away from me. As they turned away they said, "Lady we can't stay. Find the guard. Maybe he can help you."

What had happened? They had planned to mug me in the alley. I responded differently from what they had expected so they ran away from me. This happened because I had protected my aura and sent out a command for protection. My Omni-Cosmic Power Channel was tuned in and made me respond in the way I did. Later I found the party was not in the church but in the parish house which was just down the street.

Protection is available. Just tap into it. I did. It works.

TURN ON YOUR OMNI-COSMIC WHITE PILLAR OF LIGHT

There is always the need to be protected in this world of ours. I have mentioned earlier in the book that the more successful you become, the more protection you need.

This is a ritual used in ancient Egyptian times to overcome negative forces around a person. Use it for a few days after you feel someone is sending you evil. It will reverse the negative condition and send it back to the person with a strength of two to three times the force sent to you. I feel if a person is evil enough to send it out he stands the chance of getting it back. I have tried this in my life and I know it worked for me.

This is why I have warned you never to send out evil, for it can bounce back if the person knows the universal laws.

RITUAL FOR OMNI-COSMIC WHITE PILLAR OF LIGHT

May-Kam-Tee—**Spirit of positive energy, protect me from the negative forces around me. I know (say the name of the enemy) has sent me evil forces or a negative charge. I refuse to accept this person's negativeness. I surround myself with the Omni-Cosmic White Pillar of Light, (visualize it as you say it). The enemy will not hurt me or get to my aura. The evil he sent out will go back to him with a powerful force which will be greater than he sent to me. He will learn he should not send out evil to hurt or gain power over a person. Keep my Omni-Cosmic White Pillar of Light strongly wrapped around me for I will be protected each day. Thank you, May-Kam-Tee. So let it be.**

Kirk saved his job

Kirk J., general manager of a large corporation, was experiencing difficulty with another man in management who was after his job. This man, Jim, was constantly trying to undermine Kirk with the top brass in the corporation. It became so bad that Kirk was afraid of losing his job.

Jim would constantly watch Kirk and he would exaggerate anything that occurred in the business to make Kirk look bad. Kirk was an excellent manager and should not have had all this trouble.

Kirk was feeling very down and came to see me for help. I felt the best way to deal with the matter was to use the Omni-Cosmic White Pillar of Light. Kirk would be able to protect himself and send all the lies back to Jim.

Kirk used the Omni-Cosmic White Pillar of Light for three days in a row. He felt his aura was cleared by then. On the fourth day Jim was called into the president's office and fired.

When a person sends out evil, it will bounce back when you use the universal law in metaphysics. I have seen it happen every time this ritual is used. The unjust one gets his just dues. I have many cases on file to prove this metaphysical law.

So I again warn you to watch what you direct to another person. Send back his evil. You do not need to accept it. The evil person must be prepared to receive what he sent out. Just as Jim was fired because his lies bounced back.

Pamela's life was saved by her Omni-Cosmic White Pillar of Light

Pamela, a young lady of 25, was in the habit of using her Omni-Cosmic White Pillar of Light before going on a trip. She had been a student and learned about this in one of my classes. She felt more secure, when traveling, by turning on this power source before she started.

One day she was driving on a city street and heard a voice say "Stop or you will be killed." She had come to a stop street where she had the right of way. Upon hearing the voice she stopped her car. Luckily she did, for a car went through the stop street at a high rate of speed. Pamela would have been killed or seriously injured if she had not stopped.

This is just another example of how your spirit forces protect you if you ask them to.

My father was saved by help from the next dimension

When I was a teen-ager my father was saved by his dead mother from an accident or even death. My father has psychic abilities as I do, but has never used them professionally. I feel psychic abilities seem to be stronger in some families than others because the more open minds respond to the psychic forces in nature.

My father is a businessman and in those days had an old truck he used for his business. He was always a fast driver. He had been very close to his dead mother who had died ten years before. He was used to tuning into his OCPC for help with his business problems. He was always able to get answers or help whenever he needed them.

One day when he was returning to his business with a truckload of merchandise, he was driving about 70 miles an hour which was too fast for his old truck to travel. All at once he heard his mother's voice say to him, "Sam take your foot off the gas and slow down or you will be killed." He also felt her hand on his on the wheel. It frightened him so much that he listened and took his foot off the gas pedal and slowed down. Within five minutes the two back tires blew out and most of the merchandise on the truck fell to the road.

He knew his life had been saved by his mother. When he arrived home he was white and shaky. I can still remember the look on his face that day. He said to the family, "My mother saved my life. I could feel her near me." He still tells the story of how he was helped by his dead mother in a time of danger.

A spirit that is close to you will come in time of danger. You have to remember to open up the channels by using your Omni-Cosmic Power Channel. It is best each day to tune into your OCPC so you will be protected all day. Then if a need or danger arises, you will get help instantly and keep yourself free from harm.

POINTS TO REMEMBER

1. It is possible to tap your Omni-Cosmic Power Channel to achieve miraculous protective psychic power. It is available; just there to be used at your command.
2. Each day you will be able to turn on your Omni-Cosmic Power Channel to sense conditions around you for the day.
3. You will be able to repel any negative forces that come into your vibration. Your mental state means a lot in this. It can make or break your opportunities in life as well as your safety.
4. Pick the right company for like attracts like—what you sow, so shall you reap. Start today to program a protective force around you using your Omni-Cosmic Power Channel. You will not have to fear anything at all.
5. Your Omni-Cosmic Power Channel will keep your protective barriers up and keep you tuned into your environment. If you feel the need for extra protection use it four times a day every four to five hours.
6. John was saved from drowning by using his Omni-Cosmic Power Channel each day. It was like an invisible force which carried him over the top of water safely to land.
7. When you send out a call for help from the spirit forces in the fourth dimension you will find it comes quickly and effectively. Send your protection signals out and just let the universal forces around you come to your rescue.
8. I was saved from being mugged through my Omni-Cosmic Power Channel. Protection is there. Just tap it.
9. Use the Omni-Cosmic White Pillar of Light to stop the negative forces around you. When you reverse a negative condition it will go back to the sender with a strength two or three times greater than the force sent to you.

10. Kirk was saved from losing his job by his Omni-Cosmic White Pillar of light. Jim was fired because his lies bounced back to him. Send back the evil. You do not have to accept it.
11. Pamela's life was saved by her spirit forces.
12. My father's life was saved by his mother coming to him at a time of danger. He was mentally tuned in on OCPC everyday. OCPC works. All you have to do is to use it.

Chapter 17

Using Omni-Cosmic Power for Miraculous Weight Control and for More Youthful Energy

With Omni-Cosmic Power (OCP) you will learn to program your subconscious mind to lose weight and be more youthful with lots of energy. You do not have to diet. You need to avoid some foods and follow a new effortless way to achieve your perfect weight.

OCP will reprogram you to select the proper foods with new eating habits so you will not eat unless you need food. There will not be any starvation pangs and you will do it with little effort. You will lose your desire for fattening foods and eat those with more protein and be just as satisfied.

Most people dislike diets because they assume hunger throughout the regimen is the price they have to pay. Hunger is a reaction of the body to let you know that the body needs food. Generally, people will turn to carbohydrates such as fats, starches or sugars because these foods satisfy hunger pangs most quickly. Carbohydrates, when eaten, easily convert to fat and are stored as energy in the body. Now you can realize it is so important to reprogram the mind to be satisfied by food that will be nonfattening. It is as simple as this for miraculous weight control. You can be thin the rest of your life.

Start today to think thin.

You will have half the "battle of the bulge" licked by positive thoughts. OCP power will do the rest.

YOU MUST FORGET YOUR EARLY PROGRAMMING

When you were an infant, all your fears of loneliness and insecurity were removed when your mother gave you her nipple or your bottle of milk. From our early years, we were programmed to seek food when we needed love, or assurance of some kind.

Thus as you got older, food became your security when you needed love or sex, had money problems or other worries that presented themselves at the time.

When you did something good as a child, your mother would reward you with an ice cream cone or a piece of pie or cake. Thus you were programmed to accept food as a reward. Usually it was something sweet. The richer the food the more you liked it.

Once you recognize the pattern that developed in your childhood you will realize that you will have to reprogram yourself in an opposite direction.

LEARN TO WORK WITH YOURSELF

It will be necessary to work with yourself for you will need the proper motivation to take away the hunger and try to find out why you depend on it, for there will be some emotional need you are substituting.

Do not substitute food for insecurity, loneliness, anxiety or frustration.

Use a positive approach. See a doctor for a checkup any time you start to try to lose weight, just to be sure your body is in good condition.

YOU WILL OVERCOME THE HABIT OF OVEREATING

Program your subconscious mind so you will be able to control the intake of foods each day. You do not need to have sweets each time you have a coffee break. It is just a habit that can be broken.

With the proper programming you will lose your desire for fattening foods and substitute your food desires for protein or low calorie foods.

Each day you will say the ritual which is really talking to your subconscious mind through Omni-Cosmic Power channels, knowing that by your weight loss you will become more attractive, healthier and have a longer life.

"YES" FOODS VERSUS "NO" FOODS FOR MIRACULOUS WEIGHT CONTROL

In order to lose weight and thereafter maintain your proper weight, it is necessary to control your intake of starches and sweets. Most diets recognize this factor. Your carbohydrate intake should be lessened. Your body can make energy from both carbohydrates and protein.

The secret is to cut down on carbohydrates and eat more proteins, for the proteins do not store fat in the body and are necessary to revitalize your body cells. You also need vitamins and minerals. Most of them can be found in proteins and some from fresh vegetables and fruits.

I also recommend, in addition to seeing a doctor for a checkup, that you add some vitamin and mineral tablets to your diet to insure the proper balance in your body.

I will list two sets of foods. One are the "yes" foods and the others are the "no" foods. The "no" foods should be programmed out of your diet and out of your mind in order to maintain the weight you wish to lose. Your Omni-Cosmic Power will help your subconscious do this for you. Convince yourself you do not want or need the "no" foods. Tell yourself you dislike them. If you say this to yourself each morning, you will start to believe it after a while.

The "yes" foods are high protein foods and have a high vitamin and mineral content. These foods will keep you well and help your body keep off the fat.

"YES" FOOD LIST (Low Calorie) FOODS

Eggs, Cheeses (except cream cheese), Cottage Cheese.

Meats—Lamb, Pork, Beef, Bacon and Poultry.

Fish—Freshwater Fish, Shellfish, and Canned Fish (if oil is drained.)

Fruits—Lemons, Melons, Oranges, Grapefruit, Tangerines, Rhubarb, Limes.

Vegetables—Asparagus, Green Beans, Beet Greens, Broccoli, Cabbage, Cauliflower, Celery, Chard, Chicory, Collards, Cucumber, Eggplant, Endive, Kale, Lettuce, Mushrooms, Mustard Greens, Parsley, Peppers, Radishes, Spinach, Tomatoes, Turnip Greens, Watercress, Zucchini and all other kinds of leafy vegetables.

Milk—Skimmed, Buttermilk, Yogurt.

Beverages—Coffee, Tea (with skim milk and artificial sweetener).
All the water you want. No-sugar Carbonated sodas.

"NO" FOOD LIST (High-Calorie Fattening) FOODS

Cereals—Dry or cooked.

Flour Products—Bread, Rolls, Crackers, Noodles, Macaroni, Spaghetti.

Rich Desserts—Pie, Cake, Pastries, Pancakes, Waffles, Ice Cream, Candy.

Rice

Jams, Jellies, Sugar Preserves.

Sauces and Gravies

Liquor, Wine, Beer and Soda.

HOW TO TURN ON YOUR OMNI-COSMIC POWER FOR WEIGHT LOSS

The power of your mind controls your body weight. You will program your subconscious mind to accept the right foods for you and reject the "no" or fattening foods.

A new mental outlook is needed for this to be successful. In this way you will be able to take the weight off and keep it off forever. Of course you can go to a doctor and get diet and water pills and lose all the weight you want to. Once you go back to your old eating habits all the pounds come back again. All your fine efforts in dieting can seem like a losing battle.

With your Omni-Cosmic Power Ritual you will be able to avoid the wrong foods and condition your mind for the right foods.

THIS IS THE WAY TO CONIDITION YOUR MIND WITH OCP.

1. Find a comfortable chair and relax your whole body.
2. Close your eyes and achieve a peaceful meditative state.
3. Say the following ritual for weight control:

Ro-Bar-Ton—Spirit of health and diet, help me to lose weight. Help me to condition my mind along the right pathways of eating. I will grow to enjoy the "Yes" foods and find the "No" foods less and less appealing each day. I will also get more and more satisfaction from less and less food each day. I will lose 2 to 5 pounds each week. It is so easy to lose weight. I am so proud of my figure. I am pleased with my total appearance and looking younger all the time. The extra weight is just rolling off, melting away from the parts of

my body where there is too much. I will be the size and shape I want to be. I can see in my mind exactly what I will look like in a short time—slender and shapely. I will stay in perfect health and keep my ideal weight. Thank you, Ro-Bar-Ton, for your help. So let it be.

4. Say this ritual five times each morning. Your OCP ritual will go into action and work on your subconscious mind. It will help you achieve all you believe you can do.

Soon you will find an orange or melon more appealing to your taste buds and reject the rich pie or cake. You will feel it is not worth the extra pounds to eat the fattening foods.

You will build a strong mental image of yourself in your mind. It will have a long-reaching and lasting effect on you.

Samantha lost 95 pounds and found a husband

Samantha was 235 pounds at the age of 29. She had never been able to lose weight. She was a chubby teenager and just gained weight through the years.

Samantha had never had a date and was resigned to her dull life of work and watching TV every night. She would eat in sheer frustration.

She came to see me for a consultation. I saw her problems psychically and told her I felt she could lose about 100 pounds if she really wanted to.

I also felt she would meet a young man after she had lost the weight and he would ask her to marry him within the next 10 months.

All of this I felt was right ahead in her life if she would only try to use the OCP ritual and create a new image of herself, to be a new person, full of life and love.

Samantha looked at me in astonishment and said, "I would like to believe this. Do you really feel this could happen to me?" I said, "Yes, but you will have to be patient and use your Omni-Cosmic Power Ritual to reprogram your mind. First you will have to cut out eating between meals. You will not need the food. You are only doing so because you are frustrated. Then sit and say your OCP ritual for weight control five times each morning before you start each day. You will find that as soon as you condition your mind you will start burning up calories and lose weight. Eat only three meals a day, and no second helpings."

I also said to her, "Samantha, each day look at yourself in the mirror and see yourself as that size dress you wish to wear. See the man of your dreams by your side in your mind's eye. Believe, Believe, Believe."

Within six months Samantha lost 95 pounds. She met the man I had described to her months earlier. Her health is fine. She is happier now than she had ever been in her entire life.

What had happened? Samantha set her Omni-Cosmic Psychic forces to work. They transformed her to be the woman she had always wanted to be, a lithe, vivacious young lady who loves every minute of life.

Life begins at forty for Bette

Bette W., a young married woman of 42, with two grown children, was unhappy, restless and 35 pounds overweight when she came to see me at my office. I picked up her frustrations as soon as I tuned in. She needed to be more than just a housewife.

I told her the solution was to go to work for she had an interest and a degree in journalism. I felt she would get a job with a local newspaper. Her husband was agreeable to this when she returned home to tell him of her plans.

Bette used her Omni-Cosmic Power ritual for weight control and lost the extra 35 pounds. Now she is slimmer and working in a career in journalism just as I had seen for her.

Bette found a new interest in life. She is also much happier with her marriage for she feels fulfilled. When Bette's children grew up she needed something for herself. She did this by going to her own career. OCP did it again by helping a person find herself in this world.

Frustrations can lead to overweight in most cases. It was the lack of confidence which Bette overcame when she tried using OCP. It brought new meaning to her life and changed her basic outlook to one of happiness.

Try it for it will work for you.

Overweight Harry could not find love until he used OCP for weight control and lost 80 pounds

Harry R. came to see me at a time when he was blue and lonesome. No woman would look or become interested in him for he was 5' 8" and his weight was 260 pounds. It was most discouraging for him. His life was meaningless at this point.

I told him he would have to look more appealing in order to get a woman interested. He decided to use OCP to lose weight. Within six months Harry lost 80 pounds . . .

He came back to see me at my office to show me his new appearance. I was busy at the time with a client. While he was waiting for me, he met a young lady with whom he became friendly. They dated and fell in love in a short time. It was love at first sight for both. Harry married the young lady he met in my office within the year. OCP power brought him love and new self confidence. He became a new person. It can happen to you too.

CHANGE YOUR SANDWICH HABIT

Most people in this country have the habit of eating bread for lunch. Bread can add all those extra calories you do not need, but will store in your body as energy.

Try making your sandwiches with something else that is not bread, such as lettuce, cold meat or cheese. You can wrap your filler in any of these items. This will keep the carbohydrates down to a minimum and you will find that you are just as filled at the end of your lunch.

You can also put a hamburger between two slices of cheese and it will be just as delicious as bread. You may want to try two slices of cold meat between two slices of cheese. This is all protein. Eliminating bread will take pounds off you in a short time. As you program your mind that you do not need this type of food, you will no longer crave or want it.

A change in your eating habits is necessary. This will be done for you as you continue to say your OCP ritual for weight control.

The results will be wonderful for you.

Start today for it is so easy to follow.

How Tony the truck driver became lighter and healthier with OCP

Tony K., a truck driver I know, had a problem of being 120 pounds overweight. He would frequently stop at a diner or a roadside restaurant and have a piece of pie or cake or some sweet with coffee each day that he worked. Calories will really pile on a person in this way, for Tony 120 pounds overweight was too much. He was so fat he could hardly fit into the cab of his truck.

He was divorced and unhappy when he came to see me about changes in his life. I suggested my OCP ritual for weight control for I felt he was frustrated and would eat constantly to forget his problems. He tried the OCP ritual and was able to lose 50 pounds in the first six months, and the rest within the year.

He substituted proteins for carbohydrates when he needed a snack, and had his coffee black. He found he became more energetic and felt healthier as the pounds started to drop off.

He found an attractive woman whom he started to date. Tony did not gain back the weight he lost. I saw him two years later with a slim, young man's figure and the new woman in his life who was to be his wife.

He came back to see me for help to see his future again. I advised him to marry for he would be happy. It all happened just as I had predicted.

Today, Tony has a fine wife, a perfect home life, and all the happiness he ever dreamed of.

Joyce was healed after she lost 50 pounds

I recall the case of Joyce W. who was 50 pounds overweight. She had high blood pressure, arthritis and some other ailments that kept her feeling sick most of the time. She drank 10 to 12 cups of coffee each day and was nervous, tense and frustrated. She claimed she did not eat very much, but could not drop a pound of this excess weight. She would eat foods that were prepared or very easy to fix. Her diet was mostly made up of carbohydrates and this was the main reason she could not lose any weight.

Joyce did not sleep well. Her marriage was not good for she quarreled with her husband over everything. She was depressed and becoming psychotic.

I felt OCP would calm her nerves and she would have less desire for food. She had to change over to a protein diet which she did, and lost the 50 pounds. On her new diet she found her health improved and mental condition improved. Her fatigue and irritability disappeared.

She looked and felt like a new person. Her husband was proud of her new figure and bought her a mink coat as a birthday present. Joyce gained new confidence. They joined a country club and Joyce took up golf. And she now had new social contacts which enriched her life and gave her a new reason to be alive.

Joyce realized that there was no reason for her to be unhappy. She was married to a highly paid executive so they did not have money worries. She had just gotten into a rut which OCP changed and she found supreme happiness and joy.

Wendy conquered her fears of obesity with OCP

Wendy, a model and client of mine, was upset about her weight. She had to maintain a weight of 115 pounds for her 5' 6" figure. Cameras have a way of showing every pound and making a model look heavier than they are to start with. She would put weight on very easily.

Wendy had to watch her food intake very closely. It was difficult because she loved fattening foods.

Omni-Cosmic Power for Weight Control and Youthful Energy 205

When she came to see me she had gained 15 pounds and could not work because of it. In her case it was serious. She was a wreck and did not know what to do.

I told her OCP was the only answer for her to control her weight problem. She would be able to eat the right foods and would not want the wrong foods.

Within two and one-half weeks Wendy took off the 15 pounds. Today she is able to maintain her figure without working at it so hard. She has her mind conditioned to the "yes" food and "no" to the wrong ones.

OCP was the answer for her.

TOO MUCH WEIGHT WILL SHORTEN YOUR LIFE

Most insurance companies say that if a person of 50 years of age is 50 pounds overweight, he will shorten his life by 50 percent. This means that if you are of normal weight you can expect to live about 20 to 25 more years. But if you are 50 pounds over you can only expect to live about 10 to 12 years.

If you think about it, have you seen many old fat people? You will find very few. It is up to each person who is overweight to keep his weight normal. OCP is the way to accomplish this.

Life should begin at 60—not end for you because you failed to control your weight, easily, effortlessly through OCP.

POINTS TO REMEMBER

1. Omni-Cosmic Power will help you to program your subconscious mind to lose weight and be more youthful with lots of energy.
2. You do not have to diet. Just avoid some foods and follow a new effortless way to achieve your perfect weight.

3. OCP will reprogram you to select the proper foods with new eating habits so you will not eat unless you need food. You will lose your desire for fattening foods and eat those with more protein, and be just as satisfied.
4. From our very early years we became programmed to seek food when we need love or assurance of some kind. Thus as you got older, food became your security when you needed love, sex, had money problems or other worries that presented themselves at the time.
5. You were programmed to accept food as a reward. Usually it was something sweet. The richer the food, the more you liked it.
6. Once you recognize the pattern you developed in your childhood you will realize that you will have to reprogram yourself in an opposite direction.
7. Do not substitute food for insecurity, loneliness, anxiety or frustration. Use a positive approach. See a doctor for a checkup before you start to lose weight, to be sure your body is in good condition.
8. The power of mind controls your body weight. A new mental outlook is needed for OCP to be successful. In this way you will be able to take off weight and keep it off forever.
9. With your OCP ritual you will be able to avoid the wrong foods and condition your mind for the right foods.
10. Say the OCP ritual for weight control five times every morning and it will go into action and work on your subconscious mind. It will help you achieve all you believe you can do.
11. You will build a strong mental image of yourself in your mind. This will have a long reaching and lasting effect on you.
12. The secret is to cut down on carbohydrates and eat more proteins for the proteins will not store fat in the body and are necessary to revitalize your body cells.
13. Try making your sandwiches with something else besides bread. This will keep the carbohydrates down to a minimum and you will get as much satisfaction from the food.
14. OCP can do wonders for you.

15. Start today to create a new, more self-confident person, one that you have always wanted to be.
16. Too much weight will shorten your life. Life should begin at 60, not end for you then.
17. Let OCP show you the way to a new and better figure and life.

Chapter 18

Omni-Cosmic Psychics Can Release Your Full Mental Powers for Greater Health and Success

Omni-Cosmic Psychics is a powerful force that causes miracles to happen to you. By now you are ready to learn to focus this powerful force from within your being to seek out whatever you wish to accomplish in the universe. It will realize your full mental powers so you will procure success, health and happiness in your life.

It makes life worth living.

Start to believe and accept in your mind that you will be the person you have always wanted to be or like someone else successful you have admired. It can happen to you now.

Don't wait, but have the courage to try it. The results are rewarding. You will wonder why you did not try it sooner.

Be ready to change your life now.

MEDITATION IS VERY IMPORTANT

If you wish to build up your personal power within it is necessary for you to learn the art of meditation, for it opens a way for you to talk to your subconscious mind.

Your conscious mind acts as a filter to the subconscious mind. It is important if you wish to talk to your subconscious mind to put the conscious mind asleep. This is done by meditation for it is the way of talking to the subconscious mind.

Problems that occur in your life may become mental blocks. They may be lodged in the subconscious mind for this is the place where we store our past. It is the mental blocks that keep us from getting what we want in life. They make us unsure, insecure and afraid to move ahead.

It is also necessary to free ourselves from guilt complexes. Mentally you should begin to feel worthy of success and good health and that you are capable of attaining your goals in life.

The only difference between a wealthy, successful person and one who is not, is that one believes he can be and the other does not. Doubts can hold you back in life. Erase them and you have all the obstacles out of your path so you can move ahead in a positive manner. Success, love, good health are there for you.

SHOW THE RIGHT REACTION

It is necessary to learn not to react negatively to things around us. I do this when I drive my car each day. If another driver gets in my way or does something selfish on the road, I send him love and do not let it upset me. I have found my day will go better and I do not feel hostility at the end of the day towards other drivers or my fellow man.

Have you seen a person who gets mad at everything around him? His day starts out with a problem at breakfast. Then he misuses everyone that gets in his way. He slams the door as he leaves his house. He slams his car door. He curses all the other drivers on the road. Then at the office he is very critical and sharp towards his secretary. He is reacting because he has a mental block, so everything disturbs him.

When you get upset, neutralize the anger. Send back love to the person instead of animosity. In this way you do not build up mental blocks in your subconscious mind.

When you send poisonous ideas or emotions to yourself all day, you actually block the positive things in life. You will receive negative results.

Your mind creates the future. If you feel you have bad luck, it is your mental outlook that created it.

RITUAL FOR RIDDING YOURSELF OF NEGATIVE THOUGHTS

Use this ritual whenever you have the need for clearing out any negative ideas that may come up during the day or the week. If you clear them up quickly, you will not develop any mental blocks.

We do live in a negative world. Newspapers, radio, TV, our friends, or fellow workers can be negative at times and we can react because of these associations or ideas. Sometimes we do not realize the effect our environment has upon us.

THIS IS THE RITUAL TO USE

1. Find a comfortable chair to sit in. Your body should be comfortable so you can relax fully.
2. Visualize your body as being full of a dark substance. See this dark substance going out of your body through your feet. See it going out of your house into the street and down into a gutter.
3. Next see your body completely emptied of the dark substance. Then visualize clear water cleansing your whole body going in through your head coming out of your feet. It will be going in a downward motion cleansing the whole body.
4. Feel that your whole body has been cleansed with clear water. You will know all your negative thoughts have gone out of the house down the drain in the street.

SAY THE FOLLOWING RITUAL AS YOU DO THIS

Thr-Ro-Ten—Spirit of cleansing power of the universe, give my body and mind a good cleaning. I do not want to gather negative thoughts. My mind will be filled with positive ideas and I will be successful, healthy and a credit to my family, friends and community. I will be a credit to the nation I live in. I will be the person I want to be. I will be positive in all I do. Thank you, Thr-Ro-Ten. So let it be.

THE POWER OF SUGGESTION IS LONG-LASTING

As a child I was told by my mother that if I got my feet wet or was in a draft, I would get a cold. Twenty years later when I get my feet wet or get in a draft, I immediately get the sniffles and start to feel a cold coming on. My mother gave me some powerful suggestions, so much so that my body reacts to them unless I change them. These suggestions feed into the subconscious mind which controls all of your bodily functions. You react to whatever you have been told or conditioned mentally and accepted to be the truth.

If you have some ideas that are causing poor health, or lack of success due to past conditioning, you should feed your subconscious mind the truth. Change your negative thinking today. You can bring positive results into your life.

Illness starts in the mind. Then it affects the body. My mother was unhappy because she was adopted. She never knew her real parents. She felt her adopted mother did not like her. This really ate away at her all through her life. It actually poisoned her body. She developed crippling arthritis. In order to overcome this condition she needed to forgive her stepmother. She would not and her condition became worse as her hatred grew.

Her health went downhill. I told her again to forgive her mother. By now she was so ill she agreed to do so. Within eight months her arthritic condition showed improvement. She regained her health when she replaced love for hate, for she finally realized she was hurting her health by all of this. By the end of a year she was well again.

Release your hatreds. Replace them with love. You will find it is worthwhile to think differently. Find the best in the world. Do not seek out ugly or negative ideas.

Start today to believe in yourself. Omni-Cosmic Psychics will do wonders for you.

LOOK AT YOURSELF IN A NEW WAY

I feel you need to get in the right mental state before you start any form of meditation, for it will be more effective. You need to love and respect yourself. This will not be possible if you have feelings of guilt inside you. If you feel you are not the person you want to be, you will not feel you deserve any rewards of meditation. It is necessary to see yourself in a new way.

If you dislike your body, you cannot be healthy. Hate is a negative force and beauty and good health are positive energies.

Eve looked 20 years younger

I know a woman named Eve, in one of my clubs, who is in her late 40's but looks 20 years younger. She does not have a line on her face and has the look and figure of a woman in her late 20's.

One day I asked Eve, "How do you look so young? Your daughter looks like your sister." She answered, "Ann, I diet and meditate daily and I imagine I am 20 instead of 40. I have not surrendered to middle age. My mind and body think I am 20 so I look it. I have slowed down the aging process by my thinking. This is my secret."

I knew what she meant immediately. She is a beautiful person and also has a beautiful spirit within. This is the secret to eternal youth. I know she is right. She is the living example of this mind power.

Follow Eve's advice. If you want to be young and not lose your youthful figure and face, you will have to like yourself and others around you. This will keep you young in spirit and you will never age.

MEDITATION IS THE KEY TO WHAT YOU SEEK IN LIFE

Meditation is the way to turn on your Omni-Cosmic Psychics. It can heal you or develop your psychic ability. You may want to achieve a peaceful state of mind. You can develop spiritually. You can overcome habits that are holding you back from success. You may want to contact a loved one in the spirit world.

METHOD TO ACHIEVE YOUR MEDITATIVE STATE

1. Sit in a comfortable chair with your two feet on the floor.
2. Close your eyes.
3. Completely relax your whole body from your head to your toes. Think of each area and tell yourself it is relaxed and it will be.
4. Take five deep breaths and as you do the following:
   Count 1 and visualize the Number 5 -- breathe
   " 2   "   "   "   4 -- "
   " 3   "   "   "   3 -- "
   " 4   "   "   "   2 -- "
   " 5   "   "   "   1 -- "

   You will find yourself slipping into a relaxed state of mind.
5. Draw in your mind's eye (visualize mentally), a white screen and imagine what you want on it.

Example:— See yourself with that new job.
See yourself with the winning lottery ticket.
See yourself with a new man in your life.
See yourself healed of a condition you have been troubled with for a long time.
See yourself with a new figure and looking years younger.

Sit for ten minutes each day. Imagine what you want to create in your life. It is your Omni-Cosmic Psychics in motion and it is achieved by meditation.

You will be surprised at what happens in a short time. What you imagine will come to pass.

OMNI-COSMIC PSYCHICS MAY BE EXPERIENCED

When some people use my meditation method they feel a vibratory sensation which will pull the body from side to side or backward or forward. This may become a circling motion within the body. Do not worry for it is the psyche working on the body.

Other people may feel a coolness upon the forehead or head area. Some may feel a coolness in the lower part of the spine. Others may feel a vibration running up the body ending in a sensation of fullness in the head.

If you feel a sensation in the eyes there may be a healing taking place. You may hear a voice talking to you in your head. You may feel the presence of a spirit loved one.

Whatever comes through, it is Omni-Cosmic Psychics at work bringing you vibrations and letting you know your meditation is working for you.

HOW TO REJUVENATE YOUR BODY AND MIND THROUGH OMNI-COSMIC PSYCHICS

Omni-Cosmic Psychic power is the life force that is within you and in the universe. It is in every breath you take. It is in your brain and the cells in your body. It gives you the spark to go to action in life.

When you were born, the doctor spanked you to bring breath to you to begin your life on this plane of existence.

It is wise to practice deep breathing and do some exercising everyday.

USE THESE OMNI-COSMIC BREATHING EXERCISES EVERY DAY

1. Breathe very deeply and hold your breath for a count of six.
2. Give yourself the following suggestions. Say this after releasing each breath.
3. Do this five times for best results.

I am releasing Omni-Cosmic Psychic power to every cell in my mind and body.

I am keeping my body in rhythm with the universe.

I know that I will keep my mind, body and the forces of the universe in tune with me. In this way I will not become ill or distressed mentally.

I enjoy life. I am happy and joyful with the world and the people around me.

I enjoy perfect health.

I enjoy each day on this plane of life that I live.

Nothing negative will come near me or harm me in any way.

After using these suggestions you will feel great and ready to accomplish great things.

LIVE YOUR LIFE TO THE FULLEST

It is best to keep an orderly schedule with your mind and body. Exercise each day for 10 minutes. Do some deep-breathing exercises and meditation for another 10 minutes. Eat your meals at a regular time each day. Sleep at least 7 hours a day. If you must drink, do not exceed 2 drinks a day. If you must smoke, smoke only 5 cigarettes, spaced through the day. Think and believe you are the healthiest and happiest person in the universe and you will be.

When your mind and body are in harmony with life you will find you will not become ill. The cells in your body respond to your thinking. Try to eat natural, organic foods to keep your body as pure as possible. Processed foods do not help keep your body working properly.

When you become harmonious with your family, friends and your environment you will find life is worth living. You will be living your life to its fullest.

How greed killed Fred

Fred K., a man of 60, made a lot of money by investing in real estate in my local area. He bought property cheaply in the 1930's during the depression and later sold in the high market of the late 1960's. He was now worth well over a million dollars. All of his life he and his wife had struggled and had gone without many luxuries because Fred was a miser.

Fred felt that if he spent the money he had accumulated he would die. He came from a poor immigrant background and made all of his money by his shrewd land investments. He programmed his mind to believe this.

One day, after three years, his wife won out. She finally persuaded him to take a trip abroad and spend some of his money. By now he was 63 and ready to start living a little. If he waited too long, it would be too late to enjoy his fortune.

His wife was so happy. Now she could have some use of his million dollars. The day they were supposed to leave for Europe, Fred had a heart attack and died before they went to the airport.

What had happened? Fred had programmed his mind to believe that if he spent some of his money he would die, and he did. Negative thinking actually killed him.

Ricky became an executive by turning on his Omni-Cosmic Psychics

Ricky Y. was an office clerk in a large manufacturing plant. He was in an office with 52 other employees, drawing a very low salary. He had been a student of mine in the past and each day he used my meditative ritual. He visualized himself as head of the office with a title and making a salary five times what he was making at the time.

One day he came up with an idea that he presented to the president on how to speed up some work in one area of the office. It was so good that he was promoted to head of accounting. Within a year the office manager left for a new job and Ricky was selected to head the office.

Ricky believed he could do the job and would get it. His mind created the position so it opened up for him. Today, after two years, Ricky is making the salary he saw in his mind during his meditation.

It works and it is so simple.
Just give it time to materialize.

Harry's ulcer is healed

Harry S., a salesman for a drug company, was unhappy and disgusted with his job. The man he worked for was constantly criticizing all he did. Harry was trying to use some positive approaches to sales and his boss would knock him down each time.

Harry developed ulcers and would go to work shaky, fatigued from lack of sleep and disgusted with the world. He wanted to quit, but because of his mortgage and bills it would be impossible. Harry felt he had to stick it out.

He came to see me for help! What should he do with the job? Would his health improve? I felt that he should seek a new sales job. I told him to check the newspapers for within the next two weeks a job would appear in it. I felt that he would be hired immediately and that new job would change his attitude and his health would improve.

Harry checked the newspapers for the next two weeks and one day the ad appeared. It was a job Harry wanted in sales, with more responsibility and more money. He went for the interview and was hired within the week.

Now Harry goes to work in a happy frame of mind with a better atmosphere and a medical checkup showed his ulcer had disappeared completely. His emotional state had been making him ill. Now he is calm and happy with more prestige than ever.

He is no longer shaky or upset each day. It was his dislike for the badgering from his employer in the past that made him ill. Harry is doing a great job for he has the talent and has been given the chance to show it.

When he started to enjoy his job it had a healing effect on his mind which affected the cells in his body and Harry's ulcer was cured.

Dick gets rid of his migraine attacks

Dick B. had a hectic job. Every Wednesday he had the payroll to do for 50 employees. It had to be completed by noontime. He felt he could not take the stress. He would develop a migraine attack every Wednesday morning. Somehow he got through the day, but it was hard on his nerves. He had never suffered from his health problem until he took this job. It seemed as if he was not going to survive the way his health pattern was going.

I recommended he try my meditation ritual before going to work on Wednesday. He was to condition his mind that he would accomplish his job quickly and efficiently. Dick followed my advice and has gotten over his fears and his health problem.

It was the negative suggestions Dick was sending himself that were causing the migraines.

He cleared up the mental block he had with his work and his health changed too.

Jason gives up being an alcoholic

Emerson said many years ago, "A man is what he thinks all day long." This is how you react to yourself. It is your mental attitude and your reaction to life that make you what you are. Many people escape into alcoholism because they lack confidence in themselves and feel the world is against them.

A lady came to see me one day about her son, Jason, who was an alcoholic at the age of 25. I told her not to give him the money for the liquor for she was contributing to his problem.

She told me that he would always promise to reform each time he needed money so she would feel sorry for him and give it to him and later in the day he would come home drunk. He could not hold a job and was constantly in and out of work.

Somehow she had to reach him. Jason would say to her, "I am no good. No one wants to hire me. No one wants to love me." Alcohol put him into a world where he was boss and had control of the situation.

He was king for a day when he was drunk. Alcohol gave him a false sense of confidence which did not last when he sobered up the next day. He would drink until he collapsed. I felt he would ruin his health and die young if he continued in this fashion. I told his mother we had to get to his mind and help him to find himself and want to change.

Jason was interested in psychic phenomena. I told his mother to send him to one of my classes for I felt he would meet new people and learn how to meditate and learn to turn on his Omni-Cosmic Psychics. Jason agreed to sign up for my course at the college. He showed a great deal of interest in each class. At last he had found something that interested him.

In fact he changed so much with the new contacts he made that his personality improved. He started to believe in himself. He met a girl in class whom he started to date and began to want to find his place in life.

He tried using meditation and turning on his Omni-Cosmic Psychic Power to become an important person and find a job that would last. Jason found a job that he liked and that lasted. He became interested in helping retarded children because his girlfriend worked for the agency. He spent his spare time helping the unfortunate instead of drowning himself in drink.

Jason became a responsible citizen. Omni-Cosmics again proved it is the key to becoming the person you want to be. Jason found success in life and no longer needs alcohol for a boost each day.

POINTS TO REMEMBER

1. Omni-Cosmic Psychics is a powerful force that causes miracles to happen to you. It will realize your full mental powers so you will have success, health and happiness in your life.

Releasing Your Mental Powers for Health and Success 221

2. Start to believe and accept in your mind that you will be the person you have always wanted to be or like someone successful whom you admire. It can happen to you.
3. If you wish to build up your personal power within, it is necessary for you to learn the art of meditation, for it opens a way for you to talk to your subconscious mind.
4. Your conscious mind acts as a filter for the subconscious mind. It is important if you wish to talk to your subconscious mind to put the conscious mind asleep. This is done by meditation.
5. Problems that occur in your life may become mental blocks. They may be lodged in the subconscious mind for this is the place where we store our past. It is the mental blocks that keep us from getting what we want in life. They make us unsure, insecure and afraid to move ahead.
6. It is also necessary to free ourselves from guilt complexes. Mentally you should begin to feel worthy of success and good health and that you are capable of attaining your goals in life.
7. The only difference between a wealthy, successful person and one who is not is that one believes he can be and the other does not. Doubts can hold you back in life.
8. When you send poisonous ideas or emotions to yourself all day, you actually block the positive things in life. You will receive negative results.
9. Your mind creates the future .. As Emerson said, "A man is what he thinks all day long." If you feel you have bad luck, it is your mental outlook that created it.
10. Use my cleansing ritual to clear out negative ideas that come up during the day or the week. If you clear them up quickly, you will not develop any mental blocks.
11. There are many things in your environment that have a negative effect on you. You have to cancel these out of your mind.
12. The power of suggestion is long-lasting. You will react to whatever you have been told or conditioned mentally and accepted as the truth.
13. Illness starts in the mind in most cases and then it affects the body. Release your hatred. Replace it with love. You will find it is worthwhile to think differently. Find the best in the world.
14. You need to get in the right mental state before you start any form of meditation, for it will be more effective. You need to love and respect yourself.

15. If you dislike your body, you cannot be healthy. Hate is a negative force and beauty and good health are positive energies.
16. Meditation is the way to turn on your Omni-Cosmic Psychics. It can heal you or develop your psychic ability. You may want to achieve a peaceful state of mind. You can develop spiritually. You can overcome habits that are holding you back from success. You can also contact a loved one in the spirit world.
17. Omni-Cosmic Psychic Power is the life force that is within you and in the universe. It is in every breath you take. It is in your brain and the cells in your body. It gives you the spark to go to action in life.
18. Start today—believe in yourself. Omni-Cosmic Psychics will work wonders.

Chapter 19

Using Omni-Cosmic Telepathic Power to Reveal Hidden and Secret Things to You Automatically!

Omni-Cosmic Telepathic Power will reveal the secrets of a person's mind by just tapping it. You will be able to read the hidden secrets of the mind of anyone near you once you learn to use it.

You will be able to know the innermost secrets of people in the next room or many thousand miles away or even what a person is thinking when you talk to him on the telephone. With this psychic power you will be able to send telepathic messages to anyone, even to people you have never met, no matter what the distance is.

You will learn to put a shield around your mind so no one can tap it if you don't want him to. You will be able to tap into time and space and contact your loved ones for answers to problems and for their guidance in your life ahead. You will be able to contact the great minds of the past, now in the spirit world, for help in furthering your career or helping mankind in some way.

You will be able to know what is going to happen before it does through your new found psychic powers.

It takes little time to master this psychic ability and you do not need to use any special equipment except your own mind. Once you have mastered it, it will become as easy as turning on a faucet for a glass of water. You think about it and then it happens.

It will be ever available for you—always there at your command.

Start to develop this power today and next week you will be going full force and finding out hidden and secret ideas that can bring you love or make you a fortune. It is worth the effort. Try it—you will be happy you did.

HOW TO TAP INTO YOUR POWER SOURCE TO KNOW THE SECRET AND HIDDEN THINGS IN A PERSON'S MIND

The first step in tapping the knowledge of secret and hidden things in a person's mind is to pick a quiet time of day and a place in your home to relax that gives you good vibrations. This would be the right place for meditation, to carry on your psychic activities and to get the privacy you need.

STEPS TO DEVELOP OMNI-COSMIC TELEPATHIC ABILITY

1. Lie down so you can relax in your meditation room in your house.
2. Close your eyes and feel relaxed all through your body.
3. Let your mind go blank. This will put your mind in a passive stage so it will let go of the conscious mind and allow the subconscious mind to work at this time.
4. Visualize your mind as being full of a dark foggy mist.

Using Omni-Cosmic Telepathic Power to Release Secrets 225

5. Next visualize a golden light starting at the top of your head as a small dot, and then visualize it as expanding and illuminating the whole head which will clear out all the dark mist within the head area. In this way you will turn on the Omni-Cosmic Psychic Electrons that will stir your mind to action so your head will beam with a golden illumination.
6. When your entire head is full of this golden light you have turned on your Omni-Cosmic Telepathic Power. In this way you will have limitless power available to you.
7. Next fill the room with this golden light so that you will be able to use it any time or place that you wish.

LEARN TO READ THE THOUGHTS OF A PERSON NEAR YOU

Now it is time to develop the skill of tuning into the secrets of a person close to you with your Omni-Cosmic Telepathic ability so you will be able to use it at will. Once you feel you have mastered this technique use it with a fellow employee to see how he will react to you.

Start a conversation with your co-worker. While you are talking to him, expand your mind from the dark mist to a golden light which will illuminate the room. You will notice he will start to become nervous. This shows you are tapping into his mind. Try to figure out what he is thinking about or going to say to you. After you try this for a while, you will be able to learn every thought or word in his mind, before he says it to you. Pretend you do not notice he is nervous or picking up the vibrations you are sending out . .

The next step is to learn the hidden secrets that he would not repeat to you, but would hold within his mind. Fill your mind with the golden radiance which will in turn fill the room with Omni-Cosmic Telepathic power. Tune in at this time and you will learn all the secrets within his mind. The person you are working with will feel all this and will want to get away from you. Somehow he will sense you are picking up his thoughts. Act casual about all this. He will make an excuse to get away from you by now.

With this psychic power you will have all types of information at your disposal.

Remember, practice at home in the quiet before you try to do this in a public place. It will bring you many rewards. You will be one step ahead of anyone around you with this psychic technique.

I have used it many times myself with excellent results. Try it today. You will be glad you did.

LEARN TO READ A PERSON'S THOUGHTS AT A DISTANCE

Now you are ready to practice picking up a person's thoughts at a distance. Go to your meditation room. Turn on your Omni-Cosmic Telepathic Power by imagining in your mind that this golden light is expanding to the location where your friend is.

For example: you want to contact a friend in California. Visualize the State of California and then narrow it down to the city where he lives and then see him flooded in your golden light. In this way you have zeroed in on him. Now is the time to try to read his mind. Then call him up on the telephone and see if he says he was just thinking of you. Repeat something that you picked up that was on his mind and you will amaze him and also test yourself as to your accuracy.

You will find it is possible to pick up thoughts of the person when you are on the telephone too. Practice this for a week or so until you find you can do it effectively. I suggest calling local people at first so you will not run up your telephone bill.

BUILD A MENTAL WALL AROUND YOUR MIND SO NO ONE CAN PENETRATE IT

Now you are ready to use another technique to build a mental wall of golden light around your mind so that your thoughts cannot be picked up by another. This will keep your secrets within your mind. No one will be able to hurt you or steal any of your original ideas. You will have complete privacy mentally.

THIS IS THE METHOD OF BUILDING YOUR MENTAL WALL IN YOUR MIND

1. Lie down in your meditation room.
2. Close your eyes and relax your whole body from your head to your toes.
3. Fill your head with the golden light. Do not let the light go outside the head, but command it to stay within as your power and protection source.
4. Visualize a mental wall surrounding your head area. This will hold the golden light within the head and mind area so it will not leak out. In this way no one can tap into your mind and steal your ideas, and you can keep your secrets to yourself. The mental wall will hold in the golden radiance of light and you will be invulnerable.

Use this psychic power source before going to sleep so no one will be able to program your mind to his way of thinking or to pick up your thoughts while you are sleeping.

When I was researching old manuscripts, I found that the ancient Egyptians and Tibetans used this form of Omni-Cosmic Telepathic Power. Only people in authority knew about this kind of psychic knowledge. This is why so few could overpower the leaders in ancient times. The ones that knew the power were the ones who conquered and became great men of history.

Learn today to guard the secrets of your mind. They are most valuable if you are a scientist or an inventor. You would not want another person to steal an experiment or an invention and take the credit away from you after you did all the work.

Build that wall of golden light around yourself each night and you will become a powerful individual.

Jennifer was saved from a tragedy by using her Omni-Cosmic Telepathic Power

Jennifer W., a student in one of my psychic classes, started to date a young man named George whom she had just met. One day in one of my classes I showed my students how to use their Omni-Cosmic Telepathic Power to find out another person's thoughts.

Jennifer practiced this technique and one day she used it on her new boyfriend. She was startled to learn that George had been in jail for rape for the last six months and was an escaped convict. He had been very secretive about his past with her. She had felt psychically he had been holding back something about his past. Now she knew she was right about this. She was also frightened about this information.

What should she do? She remembered she had a friend on the police force. He was the one to contact about this. He checked to verify that George was a fugitive from justice and had him picked up and put back into prison. George did not realize that Jennifer had turned him in, which was the best way to treat a matter of this kind.

Jennifer felt she had been saved from a tragedy for George had other plans about them, but did not have the opportunity to carry them out. OCT power could have definitely saved her life, for if

George had tried to rape her and she had resisted she could have been murdered.

Learn today to develop your mental powers within.
You will find they are very powerful and you will be protected.

Lawrence protects his mind from being tapped by a fellow employee

Lawrence K., an engineer for a large corporation in my area, was coming up with many new designs and ideas at work. Before he would get a chance, a co-worker, Harry, would go to the boss and capitalize on them, even though Lawrence did not reveal any information to him. Actually, his co-worker was tapping Lawrence's mind to do this.

Lawrence told me this when he came in for a psychic session with me at my office. I told him to use OCT power to build up a mental wall in his mind so the other man would not be able to steal his valuable ideas. It was an unfair situation and it had been going on for a period of three years.

Lawrence used his OCT power and did it for a week. He noticed that his co-worker was getting headaches each day. Finally at the end of two weeks, his co-worker asked for a transfer to another section in the corporation. Lawrence was successful in blocking his mind and the co-worker could not tap it.

Now Lawrence gets the credit for the work and ideas he presents to the president. Once you build a mental wall, the person who tries to tap it will feel head pressures and it could be quite painful physically. No matter how hard he tries to pry out information from your mind, he will not get it. All he will get is a headache, as Harry did.

If Lawrence had not learned this psychic technique, his co-worker would be the top executive and Lawrence would be going nowhere in his job. Lawrence was promoted to Vice President within the next year. It was only fair for he had given the corporation many new and valuable ideas. When your mind discovers or develops ideas you should get the credit you deserve.

No one can break your mental wall when you use OCT power.

Animals will respond to Omni-Cosmic Telepathic Power

Animals that are close to you can be contacted mentally by OCT power. It will work best on cats, dogs, horses or birds. Some of the other types of animals are difficult to do it with for they are not close to man like the ones mentioned.

I try it quite often with my Siamese cat, Mr. Bub. I tell him mentally to come to me or that I have some fish for him. After I use the OCT ritual, he will sit up and look at me, think for a minute or two and move to action. Something seems to be registering in his mind. If he is not hungry, he will not be interested in the fish or food and respond with a bored look. If he is hungry, he will run to his dish. You will be able to pick up the animal's emotional state. You have to use suggestions that will appeal to the animal emotions, not human emotions, to get them to respond. You have to think like your cat or dog to have it work.

If my cat does not feel well, I will tap into his mind and see how serious it is. Animals cannot speak

Using Omni-Cosmic Telepathic Power to Release Secrets 231

our language so you will be able to learn to pick up their feelings, emotions and what they are trying to convey to you with their minds.

Try it with your favorite pet and see how easily it will work after a few tries.

YOU CAN BREAK THROUGH TIME AND SPACE WITH OCT POWER

If you like a challenge to your Omni-Cosmic psychic ability, you will next try breaking through time and space. It is best to master the other techniques of OCT power first. This will give you a better chance of accomplishing it. It takes time and practice, but about 75 percent of my students do accomplish it. So if you are interested, give it a try.

With this ability you will be able to tap into what is going on in time and space, and pick up information about UFO's and life outside our own planet earth. You will be able to send out golden lights to gather knowledge for your fellow man.

With this technique you will fill the area around you with the golden light and then extend it out into the universal.

Sit for about 30 minutes and try to pick up details about outer space and things not of this plane. Write them down to check with later if such information does come to light.

Did you ever think man would get to the moon? He did. Some things that seem impossible may not be so in the next 10 to 20 years.

HOW TO CONTACT OUR DEPARTED LOVED ONES OR GREAT MEN OF THE PAST THROUGH OCT POWER

You will be able to use your OCT ability to tap into the spirit world and contact your loved ones, friends or people you want to meet to convey messages to you. It is best to do this before going to bed at night. This is the quietest time of day and the reception will be much better. You will be able to receive your information in your sleep or just before your drift into sleep. You are most psychic when you become relaxed and go into the alpha state which is just prior to sleep or during sleep.

Relax, get comfortable and fill the room you are in with the golden light. Then turn yourself back to the person's time on this plane. Then your mind will drift into a sleep state, for when you sleep your mind can go back into time or forward through time and space.

It is best to have a pad and pencil by your bed so if you awake during the night you can take notes. Also when you get up in the morning you should record whatever impressions you received during the night as soon as possible.

The spirit you have in mind will come through to speak to you and after a little practice he can give you information on whatever you have on your mind. He can help to guide your life so you will avoid some of the pitfalls that present themselves.

If you are working on a project that a spirit person has knowledge about, ask him to help you fill in the details for he can see things ahead and have a vast amount of knowledge available on his plane of life. You will be tapping into a storehouse of information by using your OCT power.

If you are a writer, let a famous author on the other side help you with your story so the next day when you awake you will be able to write more effectively.

There are so many ways your spirit friends can help you use your power source.

POINTS TO REMEMBER

1. Omni-Cosmic Telepathic Power will reveal the secrets of a person's mind just by tapping it.
2. It is possible to be able to read the hidden secrets of the mind of anyone near you once you learn to use it.

Using Omni-Cosmic Telepathic Power to Release Secrets

3. You will be able to know the innermost secrets of people in the next room or many thousand miles away or even what a person is thinking when you talk to him on the telephone.
4. You will be able to learn to put a shield around your mind so no one cap tap it if you don't want him to.
5. You will be able to tap into time and space and contact your loved ones for answers to problems and for their guidance in your life ahead.
6. You will be able to contact the great minds of the past, who are now in the spirit world, for help in furthering your career or helping mankind in some way.
7. It takes little time to master this psychic ability and you do not need to use any special equipment except your own mind.
8. Start today to develop this power and next week you will be going full force and finding out hidden and secret ideas that can bring you love or make you a fortune. It is worth the effort. Try it. You will be happy you did.

Chapter 20

Let Omni-Cosmic Psychic Power Reveal the Never-Before-Unlocked Secrets of the Ages

You have now completed your search for Omni-Cosmic truths. You will continue to discover your full potentials as you use the rituals in this book. Man has searched throughout the ages for attunement with cosmic forces. This is man's ultimate desire. By using your Omni-Cosmic Psychic Power you will be able to obtain all that a human would want on this plane of life.

Now you have reached a level where you will next want to obtain Omni-Cosmic Soul attainment. Your soul has walked through many avenues of life, through time and space in its search for perfection to reach Infinite Intelligence or God (representing the perfect state of being). It has had many joys and sorrows. Each lifetime is just another sum total of your soul's journey through time. You will grow spiritually on your way up the ladder to perfection of the spirit. Your spirit or soul has many facets and has conquered all the challenges along the way in order to grow. We progress in this way.

We live, die and are reborn. Your soul will travel many paths on its way to achieve the ideal state. The laws of the universe are the same as the laws of your own life; for every action there is an equal and opposite reaction and for every death, there is a rebirth.

The universal mind was a great architect who devised the plan of the universe. We are all essentially part of it. If you can accept body and spirit, male and female, light and darkness, positive and negative, you can accept that we all have a chance to come back into another body for our soul to progress. It is great to be a part of a divine plan.

WHAT IS OMNI-COSMIC SOUL ATTAINMENT?

Omni-Cosmic Soul Attainment is something you reach within your own being while you are on this plane of life. It gives you soul growth for when you go to the next plane it is important to see how far you have reached out and accomplished in your life pattern on earth. When you work and use universal laws you will reap the benefits. You will grow spiritually and feel a sense of having reached your ultimate goal.

Man must strive to reach a high potential in this life by finding a satisfying career, a family, a lovely home, a happy marriage and wealth. This you will have to leave behind when you pass on to the next life. That is why it is important to leave your imprint and your money to help others to benefit from your success. You also need to feel love and happiness with your friends, family and fellow man. When you have accomplished this, you will have Omni-Cosmic Soul Attainment.

When you feel contented with the world and its people you will find that life is worth living. Aristotle the great Greek philosopher said that happiness is the sum total of a person's whole existence. Man is not meant to be a loner, but to give love and joy to others in his world.

Omni-Cosmic Psychic Power can give you money, furs, diamonds, a beautiful home, fine clothes, fabulous vacations, a grand car, but remember these are only material things. Happiness is felt when others accept you and feel concerned about you. If you have this, then you will have peace of mind and know that you have done your best with people around you in your life.

Omni-Cosmic Soul Attainment can also be accomplished through knowledge. Search this out in books, works of art, music, philosophy and your social interchange of ideas with people who have similar interests. This will complete your soul's progress in this lifetime. Life will be worth living!

MONEY IS NOT THE ONLY ANSWER FOR HAPPINESS

Money alone can not buy total contentment in this world. It is the way you distribute your money that makes it all worth while. I have known several people who inherited or won large amounts of money who were unhappy after they received it.

Money is important to buy the luxuries and necessities you need. Do not let money hurt your soul's progress. Reach out each day and give to the world some part of yourself for its betterment. Give some of your valuable time to help the unfortunates of the world. You will feel pride in doing this.

Meditate each day, drawing on your Omni-Cosmic Psychic forces. Your soul will mature and grow so you will reap a fortune on this plane and in the next life, as you move on into another dimension.

YOU WILL BENEFIT FROM KNOWLEDGE OF PAST LIVES

It is possible to learn about your past lives for they will serve as lessons in your understanding of this life. Thus you will be able to avoid future suffering and mistakes in this life as well as in future lives ahead.

Your past lives are stored in your superconscious mind. They are called the "askashic records." Through meditation you will be able to tap into this knowledge of yourself. There is also the "law of karma" in the theory of reincarnation. This simply means that for every action there is a reaction. If you know your past, you will be able to cancel out karmic debts. Then you will be able to start out with a clean slate and go ahead in life in a positive manner.

To develop the ability to look back into your past lives, it is necessary to meditate. Before you go to sleep at night suggest to your mind to search out the information you want. Then you will get it through a dream state. Your superconscious has all this knowledge stored there. All you have to do is ask that it be revealed to you.

Instruct your mind to go back in time to show you the askashic records. It will come through as if it was a recording by which you can tap into time and space and see the historic events of your past.

It will take a short time to master this psychic ability, but once you do, you will find it is a valuable tool to understand what you are in this life and your purpose for being here.

I was afraid of fire due to a past life

From the earliest days of my childhood, I was always afraid of fire. I felt I would die in this way. I was told to chase fire engines and go to fires and in this way I would overcome it. It did not work. It just made me shake and get more upset.

Later on when I discovered Omni-Cosmic Psychic Power and went back into my past lives, I found that in my very last life I had died in a fire. This was still fresh in my mind and once I realized it was a past life and not the way I was going to die in this life, my fears disappeared.

If you have fear of drowning, you may have drowned in a past life. If you fear war, you may have been killed in a war before. If you fear snakes, you may have been killed by one before. Fears many times stem from our past lives. They seem to be very real within our conscious minds. We tend to remember the negative things more often than the pleasant ones because they caused traumatic effects on our lives.

HOW TO FIND TOTAL CONTENTMENT AND HAPPINESS IN YOUR LIFE

To find true happiness and your place in life, you need to keep your mind active and creative so you will see the beauty of nature, and of the changing seasons, through music, poetry, art, drama, dance, operas or other creative expressions of life on this plane. Direct universal spiritual vibrations towards other people around you.

When a person is happy he is thinking of the other person and in this way feels the happiness of helping and doing for another. A person who thinks of himself seldom finds total contentment.

I know that there will be many negative forces that will fall in your pathway. Be prepared to meet these challenges by using your Omni-Cosmic Psychic Power. You will be able to overcome ill health, loss of money, disappointments in love and marriage, business failures, emotional insecurity, negative emotions sent to you. Use the various rituals I have given you in this book and you will be that positive, healthy, happy person you want to be. Rejoice that you now have a power source at hand any time you need it.

Look around you. See the beauty of your family, your home, your friends, your environment and your country. When you do this and appreciate these things in your life you will be happy.

Develop your mental consciousness to see and evaluate things around you in an intelligent manner. Do not let emotions rule you. Take some courses in your local college so your mind will grow to understand human nature better. Look into psychology, philosophy, science, art, music and literature. Search out the areas you are interested in.

Get spiritual refreshment by seeking out a church or metaphysical group that interests you so your mind will grow and expand to new dimensions. Try to live by the Golden Rule and find serenity with spiritual principles that have been taught by the ancient masters of the past.

You will be a new person. You will feel good inside. Whatever a man can believe mentally, he can bring to himself.

Learn to know yourself. Know your powerful potential. Read and reread this book until you feel it becomes a part of your life.

Miracles will happen. You will become a master among people around you. A wonderful future is there for you.

POINTS TO REMEMBER

1. By using Omni-Cosmic Psychic Power you will be able to obtain all that a human would want on this plane of life.
2. Your soul has walked through many avenues of life, through time and space in its search for perfection to reach God. We live, die and are reborn.
3. The universal mind was a great architect who devised the plan of the universe. We are all essentially part of it.
4. Omni-Cosmic Soul Attainment is something you reach within your own being while you are on this plane of life. It gives you soul growth.
5. When you feel contented with the world and its people you will find life is worth living.
6. Miracles will happen. A wonderful future is there for you.